GETTING TO
NEXT

GETTING TO NEXT

Lessons to Help Take Your Career to the Next Level

PERSONAL ESSAYS, VOLUME I

Cash Nickerson

CNM PRESS

TABLE OF CONTENTS

INTRODUCTION

In this era of longevity, I view myself as halfway through a planned 60-year career. The essays I have assembled here were written in 2014, during the 30th year of a career that has included positions as an in-house lawyer at one of the largest companies in the United States, Union Pacific Railroad, as well as a marketing executive and general manager for the same company. Other career choices have included an associate and then partner position at Jenner & Block. They're a large Chicago-based law firm. I've invested ten years as an entrepreneur in the world of human resources and involved myself in the early dot-com days. Finally on my resume is an 11 plus-year tenure, helping to build one of the largest engineering and IT staffing firms in the United States, PDS Tech, Inc.

The collection of essays is designed around several key topics. In the first "Career Beginnings," there are five essays—that while helpful to anyone at any stage—focus on the early years of one's career. No matter where you are in your career path, these essays will help you think about beginnings. The next set of essays, "For Leaders and Future Leaders," is helpful for those who aspire to lead, and those who are leading already. The "Trends" section focuses on social media and demographic tendencies that can encourage you to think about your career differently. And, finally, "Reflections" includes essays I wrote after a significant life event, such as the death of a friend or a visit to a thought-provoking part of the world.

I chose an essay format so that the advice is conveyed in a more conversational manner and can be read in small doses, at a leisurely pace. There are endless books about careers with "do this" and "do that" lists of exercises. While there is actionable advice in many of these essays, simply reading them for pleasure will result in change. You'll be better off having absorbed their intended messages. You also may benefit from advice in the essays that I didn't intend when I wrote them—like all reading, they are subject to interpretation. If you do find a nugget I didn't mention, do drop me a note at cash@cashnickerson.com. I would love to hear from you.

Finally, you needn't read these essays in any particular order. People ask me which are my favorites. I like them all, and they speak to me in different ways at different times. I hope these essays will inspire readers to get to the next level, and that you fondly recall them from your e-reader or the paperback version with a smile.

Cash Nickerson
Austin, Texas
February 2015

CAREER
BEGINNINGS

Beware the Bucket List of Life!

JUNE 16, 2014

If you are graduating from college this year, or have graduated recently, congratulations! As a country, we need more college graduates and we need to find a way to help young people complete their education. Our future as a country rides on it.

While graduation is seen as a celebration of achievement, I suggest you view it as a beginning. As a beginning, it is a first—one of many firsts you will encounter. And as you look for a job and start a new phase in life, you may be tempted to make checklists and bucket lists of everything you want to accomplish. However, I submit to you, that a life of check lists and bucket lists, while the popular way to live these days, is in fact, *an empty life*. Throw away your lists and start really living—learn how to breathe.

We live in a world where "first" is a religion if not an outright obsession. From the dawn of our personal awareness, our first everything is celebrated. Our first step, our first word, our first haircut, our first bath, our first shoes are recorded in scrapbooks and now in a variety of high-tech devices and online forums. In today's era of social media, there are no private firsts, as Facebook has made "scrapbookers" out of most all of us. Your graduation, 33 years after mine, will be far better documented. I think I have a few pictures and a yearbook somewhere in a file called, "Memorabilia."

The "first worship" process begins at a very young age with competitions on the athletic field or as school starts. You are supposed to come in first wearing your first pretty shorts and shoes on a soccer field that has just been re-sodded. Children achieving first place are rewarded with blue ribbons and tall trophies. For the rest of the participants? Perhaps they get a red or white ribbon or just a t-shirt that acknowledges they were present. But *first* is what matters.

And it does not end there, of course, as we celebrate our first love with every artist imaginable. Lyrics such as *"the first time ever I saw your face," "it feels like the very first time,"* and on and on. The list celebrating "the first time" is endless.

There are many implications to the worship of "firstness," not the least of which is the sense that "firstness" cannot be repeated. First impressions happen only once, by definition. How convenient. While the worship of "firstness" is not exclusive to the U.S., it is certainly perfected here. This is the consequence of being a relatively young country.

So what are the downsides of "firstness?" It tends to favor first achievements and de-emphasizes depth and deep breaths. It encourages long bucket lists, which are by definition—firsts—and breeds books like 1,000 Places to See Before You Die. It also defies science because science shows we actually get better with each time we *try*. In graduate school we are taught "the learning curve." Based on the experience of airplane manufacturing, workers exponentially improve the speed and quality of production. The first plane just isn't that good. Even a world-class company like Boeing had to scrap its first five 787's.

How about this for an alternative title and viewpoint: 1,000 Things to Do With Your Friends and Loved Ones in the Place You Would Like to Die? When I reflect on my life, the most meaningful times were not the result of checking an item off a list. What do you say afterward? "Did that. Next..." Close your eyes. Imagine you're ill, probably near the end of your life and you're surrounded by your loved ones. Would you be asking someone to hand you a piece of paper with your bucket list on it so you could see which items you had checked off? Obviously, you wouldn't.

Of course, when I was growing up, the only notable graduation celebrations were for high school and college. Today, there has been a proliferation of graduations and every class from nursery school on through graduate level is met with celebration and recognition. They are all firsts, get it? With so many commemorations, it feels like there has been an inflation of recognition of achievement. Perhaps, because of the Internet, there are an abundant ways to say "Happy Birthday," "Congrats on the new job," "Nice new pic," and "Have a good day," to hundreds of folks we barely know.

If checking off 1,000 items is not important, what is? How do we find depth; how do we learn to breathe? Here are a few tips to make sure you don't checklist your way through life:

1. *Always look forward.* I can tell someone's age by whether he or she talks about the past or the future or some blend of the two. At age 22, you should be looking forward. Keep that mindset for your entire life.

2. *While you're looking forward, live in the present.* Enjoy every minute of every day. People age and rust—and we don't teach people how to age or to die for that matter. Ask aging folks if they would rather have more time— or more money.

3. *Pick your friends carefully.* There is very little in our lives that we get to choose. We don't choose when we are born, who our parents are or where we are born. On the other hand, we do get some choice about who to talk to in the playground. Choose wisely.

4. *Collect mentors.* I am 55 years old and consider myself pretty successful. But the most challenging times in my life occurred when I had nobody to turn to for advice or support. You should always have people around you whom you trust and can turn to when you find yourself going through a rough time.

5. *Find a way to do something good – as often as possible – if not every day.* It is good for your soul and the collective soul of society.

6. *Measure yourself and your progress and work to improve your performance.* I have employed thousands of people over the course of my career and I firmly believe this ability is the most single important quality in an employee.

7. *Be a great friend.* Be that person.

8. *Be a giver, not a taker.* You know the difference.

9. *Learn to forgive yourself.* You are going to make mistakes. You are human. If you can't forgive your mistakes, you will never be able to forgive others.

Unfortunately, if you don't forgive others, you will have no friends.

10. Smile. Start smiling now, because 33 years from now, you will have wrinkles. They will be evident whether you frowned or smiled in life. Wrinkles are just the result of trained muscles.

Life is a grand buffet. Now that you're out of school and in the real world, you get to sit at the adult table. You get to choose what to take onto your plate, how much to take, who you eat with, and how long you graze. But you shouldn't confine yourself to a tasting of every item so you can say that you tried the chicken masala once. Don't keep a checklist of what you will eat. Work with your friends, your family and your mentors to learn what food is good for you and what you can contribute to the buffet. As a way of life, the bucket list mentality will confine you to a diet of small plates and appetizers. While small plates and appetizers is no doubt a legitimate diet, get yourself some steak.

Six Learning Tips
from a Six-Month-Old

JULY 25, 2014

You may wonder what I, as a six-month old, could possibly teach you about how to learn. But don't you know that my young mind is on fire because my brain both develops and learns at the same time—and I learn much faster than you? Think of me as having a much faster micro processor (at least relative to my grandfather who is age 55), nearly completely empty RAM, and an empty hard disk. From a learning speed perspective, you simply cannot compete with my brain. And, my doctor says I have a 50% chance of living to be 100-years-old, so how I learn now is important. You older folks, like my grandfather, learn much more slowly and I understand that's important as well. Your brains are already complex and full of many connections. So what can we learn from each other? My mind is open. Is yours?

Here are six tips that are helping me to learn very quickly:

1. *Curiosity.* I am obsessively curious about my surroundings. I hardly ever only look in one direction. I notice that most adults tend to look straight ahead or even look down. Maybe walking is more difficult than it looks, or perhaps these people are afraid of falling. You know, curiosity is actually good physically. I sometimes have to stretch and contort my entire body in order to see something. As a result, my neck is quite flexible.

2. *Determined.* If I want something, I keep after it and don't give up. Sometimes when I'm curious about something I see, my parents will move that object away from me. That doesn't deter me at all. I reach for it again, and they move it again. Then I stretch farther and get my hands on it and then, it is snatched away from me. But I stay focused on it and I either end up getting it or my parents have to move it out of my vision. I am a determined learner.

3. *Tactile.* I am not a philosopher yet, but if I were one, I would say I am an empiricist. That means that I don't feel I can know or understand something unless I touch it. Right now I prefer tasting, but that may have to do with my teething. I like to grab and hold things---the tighter the better. And I like to look at objects from all angles. That's not the way I've observed you adults. You seem to spend all your time staring at screens or out windows. And, come to think of it, windows are just screens themselves. Everything is framed for you. I hate frames. If I saw a frame I would grab it and taste it— and certainly would not confine myself to the contents inside the frame. I guess you could say that we are born to think outside the box, but we lose that ability over time.

4. *Fearless*. Being a six-month-old is interesting. Many folks are interested in me. They do all sorts of things to try to get me to smile or laugh. Sometimes they come up and just put their face right into mine. I don't blink and I am not afraid. I just breathe and observe. My learning would be impeded if I had fear and stress. My open mind doesn't know what it should fear, so I take it all in.

5. *Mimic*. Because I am not yet obsessed with myself, I study everything others do. I am the opposite of self-centered. I watch and mimic. I want to do what you are doing. I assume everyone I meet has something to teach me and so I watch and mimic them all. This is such a great form of learning. I sense from watching adults that they lose this sense of mimicry over time as they gain confidence in themselves. That is sad because mimic is how I learn the best.

6. *I don't care how I look*. Learning can be messy and ugly. When I am stretching to see or grab something, I probably don't look as cute as babies who are sitting still. Learning can be an ugly and get your hands dirty process. Instead of reading about streams and rocks on the Internet, I like to pick them up and study them. If you aren't getting your hands dirty, you aren't learning.

Obviously, I have much more to learn. But I thought I would share with you some of the benefits of the approach to learning that God and nature have given me. I know that it has been nearly 55-years since my grandfather was my age, but I am committed to helping him achieve an open mind, even as he waves his watch in front of me. If he is studying me as much as I am studying him, maybe he can learn like me. And by the way, if you haven't napped in a while, it also helps your learning—I highly recommend it.

(Written through the eyes of Paige, my six-month-old granddaughter)

Find Your Job Boring? #fixit—Don't Quit

OCTOBER 22, 2014

Recently, I was reading a study of the changing workforce. It was published by Zurich and noted the following results: **"Younger workers value purpose; a study by Intelligence Group found "64% of Millennials—people age 18-29—would rather make $40,000 a year at a job they love than $100,000 at a job they find boring."**

As a Boomer and a student of the workplace (See my book, BOOMERangs, Engaging the Aging Workforce in America, I reflected on my observations and career and sure enough, much of work is boring.) As I like to say, that is why we pay people to work. But the best employees don't quit because of the "boring" nature of their work. They leverage boredom into better practices and ways of doing things. We all seem to worship "disruption" as almost the sole source of invention and creativity these days. "Disruptive thinking" has to be one of the most commonly overused phrases in modern business.

Instead consider "boredom" as a source of innovation. How can we leverage the reality of boredom in the workplace instead of moving to another "gig." By the way, Millenials, we Boomers are not big fans of the term "gig." Let's examine some inventions and just see how much was disruption and what folks were doing at the time. How about starting with Albert Einstein?

Let's see, Einstein couldn't get a teaching job after graduation. His grades were average (4.91/6). His father wrote a letter on his behalf in 1901 to get him a position as a patent clerk, which failed. (It was a tough job market, just like today.) Finally an old university pal got him on as a patent clerk third class at Bern.

How tough was life for a patent clerk? He and his wife had to give away their first child because they couldn't afford her. He applied for a promotion in 1904 to patent clerk second class and didn't get it. His boss at the time said he needed a better understanding of mechanical engineering before he could be promoted. When did he publish his paper on relativity containing $E=MC^2$? The answer: 1905. That is what Einstein accomplished while he worked a "boring" job.

So besides quitting, here are some tips for Millenials and Boomers on how to deal with that "boring" job.

1. Ask yourself why your job is boring and try to help the organization adjust it. If a job is truly boring, it may be that some reorganizing of work needs to happen. Boring jobs can mean that there are tasks that could be done by a machine. We call this the law of comparative advantage. Or maybe the tasks should be done at a lower level in the organization. If you are bored, your mind is telling you, "Hey, you don't need me for this." Listen to your mind and take the time to analyze your job. Just because someone gave you the task doesn't mean anyone has given it strategic thought. Part of your job is to consider how the tasks you do could be done better. This is a great way to get promoted.

2. Recognize that your job is not the sole source of your contribution to the world. If you spend your life job-hopping to find the perfect use of your skills, you may never find it and may never make the contribution you can to the world. If you have a concept you are interested in pursuing that is a dream for you—work on it in your spare time. A job that gets you close may be enough. Dream jobs are overrated. Einstein couldn't get a job teaching where he could spend his time on nothing but physics. But it is arguable and has been argued that some of what he saw as a patent clerk was helpful to his innovative thinking. Einstein's patent clerk third-class job wasn't a dream job, but it did put him in touch with the dreams of others as he examined patent applications. Find a position where you get elements of your dream and then work on your dreams on your time and in your sleep (this is what Einstein did.)

3. *Recognize the value of and then engage in "day dreaming."* How about gravity? How did that discovery come about? I seem to recall an apple falling while someone was sitting and daydreaming. Did it really hit Newton in the head? I think not. But there is evidence from those close to Newton, that daydreaming prompted him to notice the apple fall, thus leading to his discovery of gravity. Gee, why did the apple fall down and not go sideways? Take advantage of gravity and put down your phone, iPad, tablet, etc. and let your mind wander freely for a change. Leverage your boredom and daydream! Newton did. I imagine that if Newton were staring into a PDA, no gravity would have been invented that day.

4. *Recognize that some boredom is part of training.* As I said earlier, all jobs have boring aspects. When I was a young lawyer, I thought I'd die from all the reading and writing, as that was what the job entailed. Those that stick with it are rewarded someday. So make sure you don't substitute impatience for boredom and just go back to finding that dream job. In the Internet era, so many young folks have the impression, via social media, that wealth is easier to attain than it actually is. If you are unsure about advancement, check with your organization about how long you should expect to be in a particular position. Having clear and reasonable expectations for progress is a very good thing for you to have. Your organization should respect you for that.

5. *Boredom is a state of mind.* It means you are not satisfyingly engaged with your environment and you are aware of that feeling. In many ways, boredom is a choice like happiness. Find ways to make the time go quicker. Here is something I learned that sounded obvious as soon as I learned it. The more "time gulps" you take, the slower time moves. Remember, "a watched pot never boils." That is because you take a time gulp every time you look at the pot. Taking fewer time checks makes time pass quickly.

Don't leave your job just because you find yourself bored. Even CEOs get bored. Before you quit, consider the above and recognize that boredom can be a source of innovation. Some of our greatest inventions came while people daydreamed and sat in boring jobs. Take a stab at making suggestions where you can to improve not your work, but how your work is done. If your organization or superiors don't appreciate those efforts—then you can quit.

Finding Your Fortune: The 7 Career Phases

DECEMBER 2, 2014

I received the above fortune at an Asian restaurant in Dallas a couple of weeks ago. I have been carrying it around in my pocket. I love fortune cookies. Not the almond flavored sugar cookies, but what's inside them. And I bet you like them too. From kids to grownups, we are attracted to knowing what will be our future. When I was a child, this was a cultural obsession. We had the Magic 8 Ball™, which would tell us the answer to any question we asked. We had the Ouija Board™, which was downright scary—here we asked questions of our dead relatives. I recently had my palm read on the streets of New Orleans. The psychic, she was amazing in her insights. Young folks today face a Formula 1™ pace of change and tremendous uncertainty. How can we who aren't at the beginning of our fortunes help those sitting at the starting line? I see successful future fortunes passing through the following seven phases.

I. *What will I learn on this job?* *The Education Phase*

College used to be a differentiator and it still is relative to those who don't go to college. To get a job, college is no longer sufficient, just necessary. And where you choose to go to college matters now more than ever. Graduate school? Another differentiator. But don't stop there, your first job should be less about the money and more about "What will I learn on this job and how will it advance my learning?" Don't force your fortune right out of the gate. In other words, don't define initial success as the path to the most money.

The doctors have it somewhat right with their concept of a residency. Your early positions should consist of the best learning environments. Find the best place to gain training. Back in my early years, IBM was the place to get sales training. If you worked at IBM you got the PSS (Professional Sales System) where you were educated in how to ask and listen and how to handle objections. You learned the difference between open and closed probes and when to use what. You learned all this in a disciplined way. One of my early bosses once ran marketing at Xerox where they used Professional Sales Skills methods and training. He drilled PSS into me and us at Union Pacific Railroad. And boy, did it take. I still lean on those methods to this day. I am on the way to a sales call right now at 55 years old. I am confident. Why? PSS III sales training. Lean your early career choices towards learning. Don't sit at graduation in your gown and cap and consider it the end of school and learning—treat it as the beginning.

II. Where is the fascinating work happening? The Put Me In Coach Phase

After your educational phase, where you advance your skills training, you should seek and chase the most interesting work. You should feel like the famous song, Centerfield, "Put Me in Coach, I'm Ready to Play." If you are a programmer, where is the most interesting programming happening? That work may be taking place in a large company or a smaller one. Is there a correct choice? Yes and no.

On the "yes" side, all career work involves marketing yourself. And let's just say, it's easier to convince folks that you had a bigger role in a small project at a big company, than to convince folks that the small company where you worked was bigger than it really was. In other words, it is generally easier to move from a bigger company to a smaller one. In this phase of your career you want to ply and advance your skills in a project environment. Your bias here in making a career decision is again less about money and more about project scale and visibility. You want to get in the game, but a meaningful game.

III. What are my advancement opportunities? The Prelude to Power

So now you've gotten your residency or post-collegiate training and worked on some worthy projects. You should be ready to focus on how to add some management and leadership into your "diet." This phase puts you in a position where you are responsible for others. You're testing not your ability to do things, but rather your ability to both manage and lead others in projects. To put it simply, management is the art of getting things done; leadership is the art of getting others to do it.

This phase of your career will determine whether you remain a technician or you rise to the level of a manager and leader of skilled and professional folks. While there is no right answer to what is best for you, and happiness is distributed evenly among those who manage and those who do not, they are very different lives. What is important here is that your vision of who you want to be ultimately aligns with your ability in these areas. If it does, whether you decide to be a professional or a manager and leader of professionals, you will be happy. If you imagined yourself a leader and don't really have that skill set as tested through actual projects, you will be like Sisyphus rolling the boulder up the hill as it rolls back upon you. Advancement comes in many forms and there is only one CEO. Finding an environment where you have lots of advancement opportunities in many forms, ie: professional 1, 2, 3 or various levels of management will help you figure out where you fit.

IV. *What is your natural stride? Finding Your Home in the Stretch*

At some point in your career you will settle into the stretch. This is that part of the horse race after the second turn, when you settle into your trade and your calling. This portion of your career will likely feel both natural and boring. It is natural because after you have completed the education or residency phase and contributed to major projects and tested your mettle as a manager and leader, you will find a "settle in" place. It is a comfort zone because you are prepared for it. It is uncomfortable because it seems easy. You have reached a level of craftsman-craftswoman-ship. You are able to work independently, your advice is sought, you have reached that 10,000 hours Malcolm Gladwell talks about in his book, Outliers. But your career phases are far from over.

V. *Who becomes dissatisfied first, you or your company? The Beginning of the End Phase*

I remember so vividly when Steve Jobs got thrown out of Apple. It was actually portrayed fairly well in *Jobs*, the first movie on Steve Jobs produced by some friends of mine. At some point during the stretch of your career, either you or your company will wonder if it isn't time for a change. Who will pull that trigger first? This depends so much on the business cycles of your industry, your demographic, your age, the economy and an endless set of other variables. But it will happen. And whether you or your company initiates it, you will be staring at a cliff of uncertainty. This is where we need to be altering our sense of contribution and phasing our institutional workforce rather than "cliff retiring" them. The country that gets this right will rule the world for the near future.

VI. How do you pivot in a time of uncertainty? How do you handle uncertainty? What is Next? A return to Hunting and Gathering

So what did Steve Jobs do when tossed aside by Apple? He started a new company called Next. And now what is next? AARP talks of reimagining your life and career. Encore careers are advocated by some. I also like that. In my book, *BOOMERangs, Engaging the Aging Workforce in America,* I advocate the phase out of career folks to preserve institutional knowledge and reduce the burden on our society and improve individual well-being. I increasingly meet folks in this group who live like hunters and gatherers. Tossed off the career path, they put "gobs" of work activities together to keep their sense of self-worth and support themselves. This uncertainty takes a health toll and perhaps the movement from this uncertainty to new structures represents the greatest opportunity for our aging society.

VII. Can I just dabble until I dwindle? Accepting physical and mental limitations associated with age, we dabble until we dwindle

There is really no reason to stop working and contributing other than a mental and physical limitation to do so. John Adams was working and writing in his office until he died at 81. He and Jefferson died on the same day, the 50th anniversary of the signing of the Declaration of Independence. And that is what eventually happens. But you will find this group volunteering at non-profits, medical facilities and other socially "good" roles. As longevity increases, we will need to find structures for these folks to contribute. Maybe they can play a role in the modern "Virtual Villages" where aging folks help each other in virtual networks.

Whether you find these career phases in one company or more likely in many, the career of the future, not so much unlike the career of the past, will be characterized by the phases of 1) Education, 2) Meaningful Projects, 3) Advancement and Management Challenge, 4) The Stride, 5) The Beginning of the End and associated uncertainty, 6) The Hunter and Gatherer Phase and finally, 7) The Dabble until We Dwindle phase. These seven phases are to be embraced and enjoyed. When we are young we want time to go fast. When we are old, we want it to slow down. When we arrive at a single cadence, a rhythmic drum, and get in step with it and the phases of life and career, we dance.

Unleash Your Back-to-School Mentality

AUGUST 19, 2014

Every September, school bells ring again, though not for those of us in the workplace. But should they? Should an imaginary bell ring in our heads every fall to boost our productivity and success? Weren't some of your most productive, fun and powerful times during the fall semesters in school? Perhaps the structure of returning to school after summer vacation should be relevant to our work lives.

If you can't remember your back-to-school rituals, ask the parents of anyone you know who has school-age kids. My recollections of those times and the relevance to turbo charging your work and success includes these seven steps:

1. *Shopping for new clothes.* About this time of year, my mom would take me shopping for school clothes. We weren't poor, but definitely lower middle class. We shopped with coupons, mostly at JC Penney and nobody knew how to find a sale like my mom. She even named me after James C. Penney—Cash was his middle name. We would get pants, shirts, underwear, socks and even shoes there. I remember hating trying things on, I still do. My mother would tug at my shirt, adjust my trousers and argue with the sales person about fit and fashion. Fashion was not as important as fit to my mom. But when we were done, it felt great to have new clothes and new shoes. Having the new stuff always put a spring in my step, even though it was fall.

So having a back-to-school mentality means getting yourself some new threads. Grab yourself a friend or loved one and head to the mall. This is especially true if you are looking for a job and even more true if you are a "seasoned" worker. Nothing says "old" like worn or out of fashion clothes. Clothes are like armor. They can give you confidence or weigh you down. Buy clothes that make you feel good. It will show from the inside out.

2. *Shopping for new school supplies.* My mom would take us to JC Penney's because she used to work there before I was born. When we were younger, we bought crayons, pencils and rulers. The school had a list of required supplies, but my mom always went further and would try to make sure we had the tools we needed to succeed. And if we couldn't afford something required, she would figure out a substitute. I remember getting very good at sharpening my pencil with a pocketknife.

Who needed a pencil sharpener? Of course that was before pocketknives were considered a weapon and you couldn't bring them to school.

Over the next few weeks, examine your tools. Make an inventory of what tools you use each day. Keep track of how often you use each tool and how often you wish you had a tool that you don't have. Check with friends about what tools they use. Get yourself to a store and improve your toolbox.

3. *Getting an Adviser.* At school, we were given an adviser. You were always assigned someone to talk to if you needed help. Sometimes it was your homeroom teacher. Your adviser was someone you could confide in about a teacher or issue with another student and even what classes you should take. These advisers put you at ease. They were a safety valve and someone to turn to with your problems.

Back to school time is a great time to get yourself an additional mentor. Helpful mentors are invaluable. I could spend many pages discussing the best strategies to get a mentor, but basically you just need to ask someone. Be honest and say that you're looking for a mentor to help you advance in your career. I look for people who are ten to fifteen years older than me who have advanced professionally beyond my level. I tell them that I need help and I hope to be where they are in a decade or so. I offer to reciprocate in some way—payment or otherwise. Mentors almost always turn this offer down, but you should always make the offer. In general, successful folks love talking about their successes and failures. However, when people only talk about their successes, avoid them. They can't help you. If you want to study fighting, someone without scars won't be helpful.

4. *Reading List.* School meant assignments and a required reading list. Sometimes there was a suggested summer reading list. This is a list of books full of titles that someone else decided would enhance your abilities or otherwise make you a better person. What a wonderful concept this is for those of us stuck in the rut of the grind of day to day work! How can you generate a reading list? It takes a little planning and varies according to your profession. Maybe you make a commitment to read *The Economist* to give you an outside perspective on the U.S. Pick at least some books that have nothing to do with your field. How about *The Adventures of Huckleberry Finn*, any Shakespearean play and at least one article from *Harvard Business Review*? Mix it up, but create a list. One year I read Mark Twain's complete works. What a great year! Go look at some recommended reading lists online. Consider a few titles on *The New York Times* bestseller list.

5. *Goals.* In school goals are set for you. By specific deadlines and the end of the semester, you are supposed to have completed all the given assignments. These are firm deadlines because you either complete the work or you don't. I once overheard a graduate student in an accounting course ask for an extension on a project... then a paper... then a test. I remember the accounting professor first giving him some latitude and then eventually saying, "Ok, but you do understand there is an end to this which will come." Clearly that student came from a work environment where deadlines weren't taken seriously. We all have projects that can drag on longer than you anticipated. Why not adopt a deadline approach. Set specific timeframes for completing your goals and stick to them. You will maintain better discipline if you know that you'll get an "incomplete" or failing grade if you don't finish the tasks by a specific date. Ask a colleague or family member to hold you accountable.

6. Grades. One of the easiest ways to determine whether you are a student is to see whether you're graded on everything you do. You take a quiz, you get a grade. You write a paper, you get a grade. You take mid-terms, grade. Final exam, grade. It is relentless. Then what do we do in the workplace? Uh, annual performance reviews? Seriously, after you become accustomed to feedback in the form of grades, you take a job and you get stars instead of grades. It's no wonder employees look at their managers and wonder how they are doing.

If you are a manager, start giving more feedback. If you are an employee, ask for more feedback. You can even admit that you're addicted to being graded and receiving regular feedback. If you can't get feedback, learn to evaluate yourself. Never wonder how you are doing, force your manager to tell you.

7. Friends. A new school year always brings new friends, and, unfortunately, enemies. But enemies can help us as well. They bring us challenge. Much of your success in work (and life) will be determined by your social skills. You need to learn how to navigate friends, enemies and people who couldn't care less about you. Your ability to navigate people will only improve if you're regularly interacting with new people, just as you did each new term at school.

When I was a young lawyer at Union Pacific Railroad, I was fairly intense. A wise "adviser," the assistant vice-president of law (who had fought at the Battle of the Bulge in World War II) told me to lighten up a little, and that 85 percent of my success would be based on how well I got along with others. Twenty-nine years after getting that advice, I tell you that this comment was right on the mark. Get yourself into some new social situations. Encounter new people to hone your social skills.

Whatever time of year it is, pretend that it is mid-August and school bells will soon be ringing. It is time to get yourself some new threads, update and upgrade your tools, find yourself a new mentor, create and execute on a reading list, set yourself some goals and grade yourself relentlessly as well as force others to grade you, too, and challenge yourself socially. A back-to-school mentality will cause you to soar past your peers and succeed financially and socially. Hurry, the bell is getting ready to ring! I'll see you at winter break.

FOR
LEADERS
AND
FUTURE
LEADERS

Summer Camp—Why I Still Attend At 55

AUGUST 9, 2014

My father always said, "Childhood is an amazing thing, too bad it's wasted on kids." I never looked that quote up, and refuse to do so to this day, many years after my father's premature demise. Between him and me, even posthumously, the phrase is ours—mine and my dad's. He said that phrase a lot, mostly when he was headed to work and I was off to do something he couldn't do because he had to provide for us. He wasn't bitter about it. It was just a fact. He had his job and responsibility and I had... well, very little accountability as is true of us for our early childhood. Summer camp was one of those activities that triggered what seemed to be my hardworking father's favorite phrase.

There was only one way to test my father's hypothesis and that was to try some childhood activities, like summer camp. So beginning in 2008, as an adult, I started going to summer camp every other year. The camp was in connection with Systema, the Russian martial art. The leaders of this style of martial arts offer immersion training every other year at a camp about three-hours north of Toronto in Muskoka. The camp is on a lake and surrounded by dense forests. I was 49 my first time there and it was an amazing experience. At age 55, I headed there for my third camp. A grandfather heads to summer camp—why? What have I learned stealing back my childhood, even if it's just for a week?

Why I Still Attend Camp at 55

1. Surrender Control. When you go to camp, you give up control to somebody else. What a healthy change for us grown ups, managerial, executive control freaks. Those of us who are managers, professionals and executives have a high need for control. I remember taking the old FIRO B test. Boy, was I off the charts on that need for control thing. You probably are too. Think about how much of growing up involves controlling yourself and others. When I was young, we were graded on it. But when you are in control, you have blinders on. Chaos you can't control, you remove it from your environment. But by surrendering control to those running the camp, you can relax, learn and breathe without fearing the loss of control. You may have some control anxiety, but it passes.

2. *Discombobulating.* The most important part of the learning process is discombobulation or disruption. Camp is discombobulating. You trade your house for a tent. You trade your Porsche for waterproof hiking shoes. You trade your television for the sounds of the woods. You trade the urban jungle for the solitude of the forest. The process of human change was the subject of a *Harvard Business Review* article I read in graduate school. The author studied boot camp, theorizing it as one of the most incredible human change processes. How do we take a sweet 18-year old who was taught in church and school to love others and now train that sweet child to kill on command? Watch any legitimate movie focused on boot camp, (not Stripes) like *Full Metal Jacket* or an *An Officer and a Gentleman,* and you will see the discombobulating things they do: take away your clothes, cut your hair, wake you up at 4 or 5 a.m. Summer camp makes you receptive to change and learning.

3. *New and unique Friends.* The best thing about summer camp is making new and different friends. Let's face it. We live in ghettos and silos that get narrower as we age. The suburbs are not diverse. And whom do we hang with? Friends from work who do what we do. Whether intentionally or not, we live more narrowly as we age. How sad. At summer camp you meet people from all over the world and the USA. Some of them won't like you at first and you won't like them. Cool. At 55, you will question some of your ideas and behaviors as folks from different backgrounds react to you or even make fun of you. Believe it or not, that is healthy for you. You might even get a new nickname.

4. *Get Reacquainted with Nature.* As we live our lives, we move from a view of nature as a playground to nature as an inconvenience. It's raining, I'm going to get wet dashing to my car. Expecting an ice storm? Both inconvenient and will I have to go to work? I have to cut the grass. Nature becomes work and an annoyance. At summer camp we roll around in the grass, hide in the dark, train with knives while moving around trees and find our way back to camp in the dark. Nature was given to us to enjoy, not dominate, manipulate and whine about. They say young kids don't suffer from depression like adults because they roll around outside. Apparently, microbes found in the earth influence happiness. I would tell you to go outside right now and roll around in your grass, but it is probably full of insecticides and pesticides.

5. *Learn to Breathe Again.* Our breath patterns are structured around our modern lifestyle. We breathe out of habit. When you shave, you breathe a certain way. Driving in traffic, short breaths. Short breaths when under stress. Count your sighs some day. I think of sighs as your body's way of saying, "Really?" At camp, out with nature, with clean air, you can relearn to breathe. At Systema camp we breathe, a lot. We breathe while we do push-ups and we breathe with all our exercises. We practice breathing and walking for hours.

6. *Rediscover your sense of smell.* At camp, there are many smells. Your senses were designed for the woods and the outdoors and they light up when that is all they have for a week. Scientists say smell is our oldest scent and is linked to memory. In our urban lives we hardly use it. What does your office smell like? How about the inside of your car? The places we spend our working lives are an insult to our sense of smell. We have white noise for our ears to make sure we don't get distracted. How nice.

I can provide you a long list of the benefits to be had from summer camp. My father was right; I couldn't articulate these as a child. That doesn't mean they were lost on me. I just didn't know how valuable that time was. As an adult, when I return from summer camp, everyone says I am different. I appreciate and look at my urban life differently. Having given up control, I am in a better position to understand the view of those I am charged with leading. I certainly come back a more aware and sensitive soul.

I head to summer camp in Northern Ontario on Monday for a week. I look forward to turning over control, learning, partnering with nature, making strange friends, breathing and re-engaging my senses. I hope you find a summer camp for yourself soon!

❖ ❖ ❖

Me and My Monk at 37,000 Feet

OCTOBER 8, 2014

I have spent the past 31 plus years as a road warrior. For ten years, I traveled as a corporate lawyer. Then another decade passed as an entrepreneur. Now I'm at eleven years and counting as President of PDS Tech, Inc. All of this flying has taken its toll, but it has also provided me with some invaluable lessons. I am in striking distance of 2,000,000 domestic miles, just on American Airlines. It's probably time to reflect on my experiences and share them with you. Unfortunately, all that time in the air has meant that I've missed out on important occasions with my children. Here are some strategies to make your travel time for work a little more productive:

1. Stay in the same hotel each time you visit a city. The number one downside of traveling on business is that you are away from your family and friends. However, by staying in the same hotel, you will be able to satisfy the natural need for familiar contact, security, and companionship. I have a great example in my life: I began my career as a corporate attorney at Union Pacific Railroad in 1985. Nearly 30-years later, I still stay at the Sheraton Gateway, just outside LAX when traveling to Los Angeles. Some of the same employees I met in 1985 are still there. A while back, one of the bartenders said, "You've been coming here for many years." I said, "You been working here for a lot of years." We both laughed. It isn't home, but when I am in LA, I feel that I am around people who I have known for a long time. I sleep better there, and sleep on the road is critical.

2. *Get out of your hotel for meals*. Ask the concierge or front desk person to recommend eateries the locals like. Take advantage of being in a different place. Get a sense of the local color while away from home. The traveling salesman lifestyle takes a physical toll. Reward yourself. Eating at a local hangout will help your budget and won't exceed your expense report. We live in a wonderful and diverse country. Don't confine yourself to conference and hotel rooms.

3. *Explore your surroundings*. Get up early and take a walk after you have made certain that you're in a safe area. On a recent business trip to Fort Lauderdale, I got up and walked on the boardwalk along the ocean. I even watched the sunrise. Be curious about your surroundings. I know this can be difficult because such trips often include long, heavy dinners and early morning meetings. But find time for yourself. You will feel better and you will be more attentive in your business activities than if you consume endless cups of stale coffee.

4. *Visit someplace historic.* Virtually every location you visit for business has a historic site worth seeing. Take time to find out what it is and go see it. Recently, I was in Atlanta and had a gap between meetings. I visited the Civil War battlefield at Kennesaw Mountain. I had never visited a Civil War museum in the South. Obviously the Southern perspective on this period of American history is very different from what I was taught in elementary and high school in the North. After I watched the movie in that Southern museum, I wasn't quite sure that the North won the Civil War. Talk about a new perspective! If you are in St. Louis, visit the Arch. Years ago, I was in Memphis and spent an afternoon at Graceland.

5. *Exercise, Exercise, Exercise.* No matter what hotel I stay in I am always amazed how few people use the gym. If you want to survive on the road, making time to exercise is the most important thing—next to avoiding an appetizer of fried calamari, blue cheese slathered salad and a steak every night. Just start walking on a treadmill, get on an elliptical, lift some weights, play with a medicine ball, stretch. Do something that involves your whole body for thirty minutes. You will live ten years longer.

6. Have a set healthy meal and eat it every night. Eating on the road is difficult because you are on an expense account and have way too many dining choices. We die of heart attacks, in part, because we eat so poorly. My road eating habit used to involve only fish until I found out that the mercury level in my body was too high. Now, I only eat a chicken breast and vegetables. By limiting yourself to specific foods, you can avoid carbs and other unhealthy meals. After some travel practice, you won't be so tempted by all those rich menu items.

7. Engage with fellow travelers, especially someone different than you—for example, a monk. Whether on a flight, at a restaurant, in the hotel or at the bar, get outside your comfort zone and meet somebody. You never know what you may learn from a fellow road warrior or when your paths will cross again. So now, my monk story: As a road warrior, I live for upgrades. If you have Executive Platinum status with American, you experience the perks that come with it often. On a recent evening flight from Dallas to Hartford, I sat in my upgraded seat, 4E, an aisle seat. After a few moments, a gentleman dressed in a saffron and maroon robe, the same hues and robe as the Dalai Lama. He also sported the same clean-shaven head. The monk maneuvered himself to sit in seat 4F, the window seat next to mine. We both looked at one another, but we didn't speak. As the flight progressed, I drank wine and enjoyed SkyFall, the James Bond movie. My monk read Sanskrit, studied and seemed to meditate. He also appeared to be staring at me—or at least I felt him studying me in a strange and subconscious way. Despite this, I enjoyed the movie, my wine, and was totally in my own moment.

Near the end of the trip, I turned to him and said, "Are you a monk?"

"What do you think?"

He replied, "I think you are."

"Where are you going?" I said.

And he answered, "To Smith College to teach."

"What will you teach?"

"Compassion and Death."

I then asked him, *"What is the most important thing to understand about death?"*

He said, "That it is natural."

He went on to explain that because we no longer live near our parents and grandparents, we lose sight of how natural a process this is. And as we try to avoid pain, we avoid being a part of those processes. I said, "So we experience death as if it was a show on demand—out of sight, out of mind." He said, "Yes." I told him instead of studying death and dying, I was still learning living and maybe if he ever wanted a co-teacher I could teach life and he could teach death.

He considered it for a moment, smiled again and grasped my shoulder, and then we parted ways. The food on American Airlines is awful, but a monk in first class? Priceless. The next day in Hartford at Panda Express I got a fortune cookie and the fortune said, "Soon you will achieve perfection." I know it was from my monk.

Life as a road warrior is a tough life. But business, as I remind folks, doesn't come to you. You have to go get it. In order to keep your sanity and your soul, sleep at a familiar place, engage with your environment, encounter local history, jump on a treadmill and manage your diet. Most importantly, make new friends. Interact with strangers— the stranger the better. Who knows, you may even get blessed by a monk. I often think of my monk and wish I had gotten his contact information. But I don't think he had any business cards, I didn't see any pockets in his robe.

Travel safely my fellow road warriors!

❖ ❖ ❖

Let Us Fix It:
Leaders, Start With Ourselves

OCTOBER 14, 2014

As the great Scottish Poet, Robert Burns wrote: "O wad some Power the giftie gie us To see oursels as ithers see us!"

It was Halloween, 2011. As I arrived at work and opened my office door I was confronted with about 15 folks, all of my direct reports in Dallas, all wearing masks that made them look like me. Now that was scary! As president of an IT and engineering staffing firm, and with my background as an entrepreneur, I dress like a techie, unless I am meeting with a client or a bank.

Apparently, part of the message was about the predictability of my attire. I have since upgraded my business wardrobe to a uniform of button down shirts and cowboy boots. But there is a deeper message here and it is a required fix for all of us who call ourselves leaders. We get frustrated that there is inadequate follow-up. We get frustrated that employees don't work harder.

We get frustrated when results don't happen. We get frustrated when employees don't get along. We tire of certain employees lacking initiative. We stay up at night and dream of perfect execution. On the other hand, we, as leaders, view ourselves as execution machines. We can get anything done. If only employees would be more like us, we muse. We see ourselves as decisive, hardworking, savvy, and street smart. We look in the mirror and see the "coolest cat" we know. Right?

Guess what? Chances are we're not seeing ourselves as our employees see us. It's almost impossible to do this for the simple reason that we control or have significant influence over the work life and salary of those around us. Do you really expect a candid reaction to how you are doing? Most likely, you are receiving flattery and positive feedback. Your staff will comment that you appear to be working out more, or ask you about your weekend plans. These are the positives we get.

How do we resolve this incongruity? We think we are doing well and they think they are trying to do what we want and we are dissatisfied. After all, as we are in charge, aren't we the problem? Remember the movie, *A Few Good Men*? Remember the line that trips up Jack Nicholson's character (Colonel Jessup) on the witness stand? A marine, Santiago, is killed when a "code red" (discipline by fellow marines) goes wrong. Colonel Jessup lies on the stand saying no "code red" was ordered and he had ordered

Santiago transferred because he felt he was in grave danger. There was no transfer; that was a lie. Tom Cruise's character says, "If you told the troops not to give a code red to Santiago, why would he be in danger?" The point is, employees are following your instructions, living in your culture and following your direction. It is probably time for you to look in the mirror with a more critical eye. Here are a few tips on how I have changed myself, so that I can be a better leader.

1. Summon staff to your office less and go to their quarters more. One of the privileges of power is a bigger and more comfortable office and the ability to have someone come to you. Get over yourself and your trappings and go see your staff. When I was a young lawyer at Union Pacific Railroad, I remember the executive VP had no chairs across from his desk. You had to stand there and listen while he pontificated. How sad. Going to see someone else in his or her office shows respect for the person and his or her contributions. I remember the old management book, *In Search of Excellence*, which was popular in my day, The book talked about "management by walking around" or MBWA. Also, walking around is good for your health. As it turns out, sitting is the new smoking. So get up and go see your employees. Don't make them come to you.

2. If there is a cultural issue that you don't like, check yourself and your top reports and support structure.

Suppose you don't like gossip and you are concerned that it is interfering with workplace productivity. Check yourself, your assistant, as well as your other high-level reports. It is possible that someone close to you is involved in the very type of behavior you find are seeking to change, and that is a sign that others think this type of behavior is acceptable. It's important that you check yourself first. Suppose that it seems like deadlines are not respected. Again, how are you in meeting your commitments and deadlines? Are your top-level reports meeting their deadlines? Culture starts at the top. Don't be mad at the lowest level employees engaging in these behaviors. Ask yourself how high does it start and who on your senior team is sending the wrong message by engaging in a certain type of behavior.

3. Smile and be aware of your mood swings. When you are the leader, people mimic your behavior. It is inevitable. That is what human beings do. So if you have good days and bad days, you will project this onto your team and your team onto their teams. Attitudes are contagious. Don't lay awake at night wondering why there is not more enthusiasm in your work environment and show up the next morning cranky because you were up all night thinking about how to make your work place more positive. Ponder that irony.

4. Inspire, don't just push and pull. Leadership, by definition, should be from the front. Great leadership inspires people to follow. Anyone can bang on the table, including a gorilla. One of my favorite leadership quotes is, "Only the lead mule gets a change of scenery." As I reflect on the high achievers whom I worked for, the ones I wanted to do anything for never pushed, they pulled. They didn't say why something had to be done one way or another. Those in charge inspired you to be superior.

5. *Be a player-coach*. Make sure you are in the game yourself, not just waiting for something to happen so you can "manage." All managers in our company are working managers. How can you lead others if you are not "working" yourself? Make sure you are on the field, not up in the box seats. Assign tasks to yourself so the staff is aware of your work style and how you approach projects. This is the very best form of training. Let them watch you hold yourself accountable and be accountable to them.

6. *Have an innovative and entrepreneurial attitude*. Recently, I received a message from someone who worked for me many years ago. She started a new job and had to talk about leadership in a company exercise (what a great idea by the way). According to her note, I inspired the following: "I quickly reflected back on my career and the opportunity I had to work under you. And many great leadership lessons came to mind. I shared that having an entrepreneurial attitude was one of many leadership lessons I learned from you. This didn't mean one had to go start up a new business every few years. But with the mindset of an entrepreneur you are continuously bringing renewal and reinvention of yourself as a leader. When you just do your job like a robot every day you don't shift your way of thinking. You need to constantly be striving for innovation and growth within yourself, which will bring innovation and growth to the organization. So again I thank you."

What can I possibly say? I was extremely touched I never said any of these words to her. But this is how I lived day to day. It was incredibly gracious of her to remind me and everyone else of the impact of leaders.

7. Be a gracious and humble leader. As a young lawyer, I was fortunate to work for Mike Walsh, CEO of the Union Pacific Railroad and later CEO of Tenneco. I was a young dealmaker, consummating and documenting mergers and acquisitions and sometimes accompanied him on corporate jets. Nobody served Mike food on the plane. These were small Hawker six-seat jets and a tray of food was generally set out for our breakfast as we flew. Mike, the CEO mind you, would ask you what you wanted and he would actually make it for you. I can replay it in my mind to this day, 29 years later. I will never forget that. What a leader!

We all know that many problems we face are caused by

ourselves. Leadership is a tremendous responsibility. Hard working people think they are doing what we want and yet we see them as falling short. Let's start by examining ourselves and our closest lieutenants first. Let's assume that we are the problem. We can fix this #fixit.

The Only Resolution You Need for 2015

DECEMBER 10, 2014

You may think of Ross Perot as an eccentric billionaire from Texas. You may remember him as the presidential candidate in 1992, the man who got 19 percent of the vote (the most for an independent candidate since 1912). When I think of Ross Perot, I think pure inspiration when it comes to sales or developing a business. He is my icon in that regard.

When it comes time for New Year's business related resolutions, I begin with Ross Perot. Why? Young Ross was an IBM salesman after he left the Navy. How did he get that job? He was an official greeter in the Navy and while serving met an IBM representative. The rep was impressed with Perot and told him to look him up after he was discharged, which he was in 1957. He began selling computers for IBM and in 1961, IBM introduced sales quotas. What was Perot's reaction? In 1962, Perot made his annual quota by January 18th. That's what greatness looks like.

What's Ross Perot's secret sauce? Learning and consistently improving one's listening skills. And it's the only New Year's resolution you need for 2015. Do this and you'll succeed beyond your wildest dreams: You need to learn to listen and consistently improve your listening skills.

Everyone thinks they listen, but they don't. Watch someone listen to you. Observe how quickly they respond. Were they listening to you? Maybe a little. Once they formed an opinion of what you were saying, they did what? They began formulating a response. They were responding, not listening. And you can see it in their facial expression. You will note a reaction in their face or by physical gestures while you are talking and they are done listening. At this point, they've formulated a response. Worse yet, interruptions happen all the time in meetings, sales calls, random conversations. But even if you aren't interrupted, the desire to respond eradicates the quality of the listening.

What does good listening look like?

I study from time to time under Chester Santos, the 2008 Memory Champion. Working with Chester, one thing I learned was memory and listening are completely interrelated. In trying to improve my memory, I had to become a better listener. I myself was a quick responder and reactor—not a listener. I was conducting a sales negotiation a couple months ago. There were five representatives from the client. I listened so hard I thought I was going to sweat. I withheld my judgment and opinion and just listened. When they finished, and the exchange included a lot of information, I repeated the key elements they wanted at the end, even though they represented different business units with different needs. I hadn't taken a single note. They were astonished and one of them said, "Did you write that on your hand?"

Listening is the secret to sales and leadership success and we got that sale. As Perot says, "most people don't listen to customers." His superiors didn't listen to him when he told them what customers wanted. They wanted ancillary services with their computers. What did he do? Built two multi-billion dollar businesses providing ancillary services.

If you don't believe me, believe Ross Perot. *The only New Year's resolution you need to succeed in 2015 and beyond is to dramatically change how well you listen to others.* What are some simple exercises you can do to improve your listening skills for 2015?

1. Open your mind and suspend judgment. The reason you respond and react instead of listen is because you have an opinion. You agree or you disagree or you think it needs clarifying. Let it be. If you can suspend judgment, you will hear things you haven't heard. Be aware of your "self talk" and shut it down.

2. *Active listening.* This doesn't mean repeating word for word what someone says to you. It means that after you have listened and after they are done, you give them back the essence in your own words to see if you are connecting.

3. *Never, ever interrupt someone.* This is the cardinal sin of listening. And it can be so tempting. It tends to happen when you are tired of listening to someone or you greatly disagree. I have seen this on sales calls—it is the kiss of death for a sales team. It shows a complete lack of respect.

4. *To listen properly, get into a meditative state.* If you don't have a meditative state, you need to get yourself one. As a martial artist, I have one. It is for me a mindset of complete focus. In martial arts you need focus or you will get hit. Maybe you can get it from yoga or study it up. But great listening is a martial art!

5. *Check your ego at the door.* Stop worrying about how smart you are or appear. A lot of bad listening habits come from a desire to show others how smart or right you are. That's good for you, but will be bad for your sales. It ain't about you.

6. Maintain an encouraging and inviting presence. Don't cross your arms. Don't glance around the room. Your facial expression and gestures should reflect openness.

7. Put down your smartphone! I know you imagine that five minutes can't go by without you missing an important email or text. Great listeners never look at their smartphone while they are engaged in a conversation. But I have seen it done.

8. Pay attention to the facial and bodily gestures of the speaker. Take them all in. Why? Studies show the vast majority of communication is non-verbal. So listening is tactile. You need to feel it.

9. Practice, practice, practice. Listening is a skill. It is teachable and it is learnable, but there is no substitute for practice. This will be the key to continual improvement.

When I am working hard at listening it feels like work! So if it feels like work to improve your listening skills, you are on the right path.

Regardless of what you think of Perot's idiosyncrasies, policies, or other opinions, the man was a great listener as a sales person. Even as a candidate he advocated open democracy with "electronic town hall meetings." He has some great quotes, but his simple, "Spend a lot of time talking to customers face to face. You'd be amazed how many companies don't listen to their customers," is still my favorite. It isn't too early to set your New Year's resolutions. I recommend this one, just one, for 2015.

So check yourself on January 18, 2015. Are you done with your annual goals? Don't put on your thinking cap—open your ears and start listening. Please share your listening tips.

A Tribute To My First Mentor

DECEMBER 28, 2014

Your first job is very much like a first, well... anything. You remember it more vividly than experiences that come later. Scientists call this "primacy." Primacy, the special impact of what comes first is the same phenomenon that teaches us to start with the positive in a job interview. The interviewer tunes out after the first few lines—or so the studies show. First mentors are like first loves, you never forget those first years of guidance and the feeling of being taken under someone's wings; someone who teaches you to fly. My first mentor, Forrest Krutter, took the ultimate flight recently and now is with the angels.

Forrest was one of the most intelligent people I have ever met and immediately prior to his death, Forrest was General Counsel and Secretary to Berkshire Hathaway. He was my first mentor when we worked together at Union Pacific Railroad in Omaha Nebraska from 1985 to 1986. In his honor and in his memory I would like to share some of what I learned from Forrest, along with a sincere request: Those who can mentor, please pick someone to mentor this year, and for those seeking mentorship, find one. It is one of the crucial steps to advancing workplace and organizational knowledge transfer in our present barbell demographics world.

I joined Union Pacific in 1985 after graduation from Washington University School of Law in St. Louis. Under a hiring freeze for a number of years and tired of paying exorbitant fees to outside legal firms, the UP Railroad Law Department decided to hire a couple of freshly graduated law students. Forrest wasn't my boss; Bill Higgins, AVP Law, was my first boss. I was 26-years old and Bill Higgins was in his sixties. Bill was fun to listen to as he was a WWII veteran. I will never forget his description of the Battle of the Bulge. Yes, I guess I am old enough that my first boss fought in the Battle of the Bulge. The fact that Forrest was my first mentor, and not Bill, leads me to my first mentor tip. If you are looking for a mentor, don't start with your boss. Look for someone a level above you but lateral in the organization.

Picking a mentor who is not in your upward reporting line is important because people above you have their own agenda with respect to you. Their best interests may not be yours. I am not saying this can never work, but it is fraught with the potential for conflict of interest.

Forrest was Antitrust Counsel and was only three or four

years older than me. During year one as a lawyer, Forrest was my guide. Forrest Krutter was one of those rare math and engineering types who went to law school. As best I recall, he had gotten a BS in Economics and a Masters in Engineering from MIT in the same year. And it wasn't challenging enough for him, as he entered Harvard Law School and graduated with all those degrees at 24-years of age. He joined Union Pacific Railroad in 1980. Forrest followed a legacy of brilliant railroad lawyers whose list included the likes of Clarence Darrow, Daniel Webster and Abraham Lincoln.

Forrest and I spent a year working together on the acquisition of Overnite Transportation, the largest transportation acquisition in history at the time. For this, we needed antitrust approval from the Interstate Commerce Commission. We virtually lived together for a year, working that transaction and getting approval. It was a year I will never forget and in which I learned many of my most important professional lessons. Forrest left after that year, snatched away by Warren Buffett who knows talent when he sees it. We went our separate ways, and I didn't hear from him again until he reached out to me on LinkedIn as Berkshire Hathaway was on the verge of buying the Burlington Northern Railroad. I would have loved to work with Forrest again.

So what did I learn from my brilliant first mentor, Forrest Krutter, smart enough and good enough to become Warren

Buffet's top lawyer and Secretary to Berkshire Hathaway, Inc? What is it that I feel both obligated and honored to pass to all?

1. *There is no such thing as a draft.* One of the most important skills, maybe a lost art in a day of email, is drafting the business memorandum. I remember my first assignments from Forrest involved some research on an issue and then committing that to a memorandum to advise the client. He would ask me for a draft and I would give him one, not necessarily worried about perfection. It was only a "draft." If Forrest found a typo or a minor issue, he would make a tremendous fuss. After suffering several kind but firm reviews from him of my memoranda, I finally said to him once, "It was only a draft. You said you wanted a draft." Forrest smiled at me and said, *"There is no such thing as a draft. You put your name on it and it leaves your office, it is not a draft, it is you and your best work."*

2. *If you can't say it in a couple pages, you haven't thought about it enough.* I don't remember 30-years later whether Forrest liked two page or three page memoranda, but he judged how much you analyzed something by how concise you could be. He wasn't looking for short because he didn't want to read, but rather that your analysis had gotten you to the heart of the issue and you could clearly express it.

3. *Don't edit your work, rewrite it altogether.* When you wrote a memorandum for Forrest, you would give him your assignment and he would sit and read it while you waited. He would then ask questions and you would have to go back and rewrite it. Rewrite—not edit? Forrest asked questions that made you focus your thinking, not add paragraphs, but rethink what you said and how you said it. So often, you couldn't edit, you had to rewrite the whole memorandum from scratch. Try that some time. ***Instead of editing your draft after you have thought about it some more, start over.*** Try this with an email. Editing can stifle your creativity and thinking. Start over.

4. *Write in such a way that your client or manager can easily pluck the essence from the memorandum.* Forrest would read your memorandum and then say, "okay, so how do I change my conduct, what should I do differently tomorrow." Many of our audience were senior executives who had worked their way up in the railroad, Forrest explained: *"You need to give them advice not in conceptual terms, but a rule or simple principle that can guide their conduct in the matter." And so, Forrest got me in the habit of making sure there were one or two sentences the reader could take and paste to the side of their desk.* It amazes me to this day that someone with such conceptual genius would insist on actionable advice. No wonder Forrest was Warren Buffet's corporate governance officer and the only lawyer on Warren's 21-person staff at Berkshire Hathaway.

5. *Humility and respect for others.* If anyone had the right to be a little arrogant, it was Forrest. But he was just the opposite. I remember we were once late for a meeting with the Vice President of Marketing, who had started his career at the Railroad as a telegraph clerk. Forrest was upset we were late and said, "He is going to kill us." I made light of it in part because I didn't respect the VP. After the meeting, Forrest counseled me on the simple principle that our education was a gift given to help others and it was about the others, not us. What a great lesson.

6. *Every day is an education.* Working with Forrest, I learned many things each day. He managed in a way that always had me looking things up to keep pace with him. And this was well before the Internet and Google—it took time and effort. But this was a motto of Forrest's and a way of life: Never stop learning. Even now, I don't like to end my day without reflecting on what I learned.

Mentorships are so important to our future. We live in a world with 80-million Boomers, 80-million echo Boomers and 48-million between them. The Boomers need to reach across the GenX'ers and help accelerate the learning and institutional understanding of the Millenials. Companies and institutions need to facilitate mentor relationships.

For the first year of my career, a young Forrest Krutter was my mentor and his teachings were foundational for my career. His greatness was evident as he taught me to write a "draft free" memorandum that was concise, got to the heart of matters and had actionable advice. His humility and respect for others was exemplary. While I have said there is only one resolution you need for 2015, the link for which you can find below, here is one piece of actionable advice for 2015: Get into a mentor relationship. Share your knowledge and wisdom and advance someone's progress. It's good for your soul and we need it now more than ever.

Post Script: My last correspondence with Forrest was in 2010. He wrote of how well all was going both personally and professionally. While Forrest Krutter died near the end of 2013, I only learned of it in 2014 while reading an issue of Nebraska Lawyer. *I am sure he is somewhere mentoring some lucky soul.*

sometimes forget that the financial meltdown had a global impact. From 2000-2008, real estate in Italy surged 85% (53% after inflation). Following four years of declining housing prices, real estate dropped again in 2012 by 4.64%. In Italy, in the last quarter of 2012, real estate transactions fell 30.5%, despite low interest rates for new housing loans of 3.5%. While there are free money policies employed in the U.S., housing and GDP continue to fall in Italy, and I believe the gains in the U.S. are not sustainable either unless we focus on research and development, which leads to innovation and jobs. There's a great deal we can learn from what is happening in Europe—a region where policies similar to those of the Federal Reserve have been in place but have not produced jobs.

In StagNation, Understanding the New Normal in Employment, I use the acronym "IDIOT, which stands for Innovation, Demographics, Immigration, Odd Jobs and Talent Imbalances, and emphasizes the need to focus, not on creating asset wealth through free or cheap money, or artificial and temporary gains based on government stimulus, but on the true engines of job and economic growth. "I" stands for innovation. The United States was once a bastion of research and development centers. Where have they gone? China surpassed the U.S. in 2007, according to a United Nations report, and has become the world's most attractive destination for R&D investment. The investment is for all types of research and development,

TRENDS

Duck and Cover!
Jobs, Innovation, and the Loss of
R&D

MAY 12, 2014

The stock market is setting daily records, housing prices are rising to wild levels, and jobs are "forthcoming." What's wrong with this picture? Has the Fed been working miracles with our economy? Only time will tell if the Fed's activity, in recent years, has been shrewd. The real test will come when the Fed completely stops buying as much as 85-billion per month in securities, including mortgages and treasuries that it must either sell or hold to maturity. But one thing is certain: the gains in wealth have not led to sufficient jobs in the U.S., nor have they produced historically acceptable economic growth. That's why I have to ask: Are monetary policies that only drive wealth sound?

Last year I visited Tuscany for the first time. The houses are beautiful. The countryside is stunning. The lifestyle is extraordinary and there is wealth, but no jobs. We from pharmaceutical to aerodynamics, to—say it isn't so—a center opened by GM in China to focus on "new energy." Where is the indignation? Seriously, after U.S. taxpayers bailed out GM, why are they allowed to build a R&D Center in China?

And you can't blame GM. You can be mad, but you can't blame them. We lack engineers. The director of the new center in China, John Du, said, "There's tremendous people capability in China with more science and engineering graduates than the U.S., Japan and Germany combined."

Where is the fear? When I was young, Russia's Sputnik's launch had us playing "duck and cover" under our wooden desks at Atlantic Avenue Elementary School in Pittsburgh. Why are we accepting China's engineering dominance and forgetting how motivated we were by the Russians during the 1950s and 1960s. I guess I'll have to leave that to social psychologists and sociologists. But can someone please explain why the government thinks asset wealth creation is the goal? We are losing the war of innovation.

If you don't think innovation is essential to job creation, take a look at the major employers today. When politicians were debating whether to let the car companies fail, the Governor of Michigan said that nearly one in ten jobs was related to the automobile. And it was the innovations related to the Ford Model T that really changed the automobile to something other than a novelty item. The Tin Lizzie, as it was called, was named automobile of the 20th century by an international consortium of journalists and industry experts. Innovation leads to jobs, not stimulus, not tax breaks, not asset inflation.

We are abdicating our future. Our lack of fear of Chinese engineering will undo us someday. Are the somewhat successful cyber attacks by the Chinese on U.S. Defense systems, recently reported in the Washington Post, the beginning? I suppose the only positive is that someday we will be able to look over wine country in California and see that it is just as beautiful as Tuscany. However, the only stems we will be focused on will be the innovative Chinese stemware made from "new energy" as we sip our wine comfortably with our unemployed children and grandchildren sitting nearby.

We need a full court press on STEM (science, technology, engineering and math) education. It is easy to say we're in an economic battle with other countries like China. But truly, it will be about whether our children and our grandchildren will be able to successfully compete for jobs. Education drives innovation and innovation is the source of future jobs.

❖ ❖ ❖

Get a Job!
Finding the Hunter and Gatherer Within Us

MAY 9, 2014

Have you ever wondered from where the word "job" originated? Etymologists often attribute the source to the word "gobbe" meaning a piece—a gob of something. When we consider modern work structures, influenced as they are by, among others, the semi-retired, who often have to piece together a variety of tasks in order to make ends meet, work can seem for some like a collection of "gobs." When you leave the full-time workforce, you start piecing projects together. At some point, those project pieces become a business. You're probably happier because you control when and what you do. You may have less security and income, but you are smiling again.

And this new work structure of fragments or "gobs" isn't just for Baby Boomers, Millennials seem to favor this type of lifestyle as well. And, why not? Farming was only introduced about 10,000 years ago. We spent most of human history as hunters and gatherers in the two-million plus years of the Paleo era. Even modern humans date back approximately 200,000 years ago. We were Paleos for a much longer period than we were farmers, and as humans, I think we miss those hunter and gatherer days. In order to get our children to focus and not be distracted, we drug them to limit the effects of attention deficit disorder. But think how important a wandering mind was to someone trying to survive in a hunting and gathering world.

Consider the popularity of the Paleo diet, focused as it is around our hunter and gatherer habits. To get a sense of the diet, imagine your ancestors wandering about eating vegetables, fruits, grains and nuts—no processed food. An awful lot of medical research indicates this diet is far better for us than a farmer's bread–heavy diet. There is a Neo-Paleo revolution of sorts in the works and it can be essential to keeping Baby Boomers in the workplace. There is a strong need for alternative and flexible work structures to avoid the loss of the Boomer expertise, especially in technical areas where we lack adequate Gen X resources.

The 40-hour work-week and an eight-hour day have been under siege for a long time, and we need to proactively redesign our laws. Attitudes and culture need to change around flexibility appropriate to our aging population and our deeply rooted Neo-Paleo needs. Learn more by reading my book, *BOOMERangs, Engaging the Aging Workforce in America*. In the meantime, get a gob.

Social Media and the Erosion of Compromise

NOVEMBER 10, 2014

Recently, I spent a night discovering that I am smarter, growing better looking every day and am more right than wrong. Then of course I woke up. Actually, this isn't the case; I am getting older and losing my hair. And, every day it seems as if my belt or my pants were mistakenly put into the laundry and have shrunk. As for the intelligence, maybe a little writing certainly has advanced my reading, but that doesn't explain how "right" I feel about everything. And yet my mind is telling me there is something terribly wrong with these feelings of "rightness." My mind knows that it doesn't get better by being right. Learning doesn't come from a feeling of "rightness." So what is causing these misguided feelings of self-satisfaction and rightness?

I am afraid I have traced my misguided self-perception of "rightness" to social media and its algorithmic analysis of who I am, who I like, and what I like. And I don't think

I'm the only person feeling this way. Are the new tools of the Internet intent on wreaking havoc on how we see and understand our world, especially those with positions counter to our own? Does the new world of social media cause us to harden our viewpoints (because they are constantly reinforced) and make us less susceptible to compromise? Are sites like LinkedIn, with their daily emails about "Recommended for You" must-reads narrowing our perspectives and hardening our positions? And if so, what can and must we—as thought leaders—do about it?

Let's consider the fundamental nature of social media. The foundation of Facebook was exclusivity; the platform gave users the ability to select friends and which people to like. You then decide to share and exchange photos, information, successes, family events and other important life events only with those people. The group is by nature people who "like" you. Get it? And then, of course, you can create groups of your friends who have similar interests. How about LinkedIn? While the basic unit of LinkedIn is not family photos but your resume, LinkedIn also stresses the concept of exclusive selection. And with LinkedIn, I can again create groups of those with similar interests. Twitter also uses the element of exclusivity, but this platform requires you say something in 140 characters or less to your followers and the people you follow. And, there's also Google+, Pinterest and the hundreds of other exclusive selection mechanisms. Take a moment and think about how much of your social interaction is conducted through virtual mechanisms through which you select your audience and your audience selects you. The honest answer? All of it. So what is the downside of exclusive mutual selection?

Let's revisit Darwin. Imagine that we had exclusive selection instead of natural selection. In the world of reproduction that would mean the world of arranged marriages and perhaps even inter-family reproduction. What kind of gene pool would that lead us to have? Let's look at the two extremes—inbreeding and genetic selection—as analogies for the thought world. We know inbreeding is disastrous for offspring because it produces genetic disorders. The advantages of genetic engineering can be debated. But there is no doubt that the question of who gets to decide these matters is extremely problematic and the risk of what is lost in the process and the irreversible nature of the such engineering must give anyone pause. That's why we should worry about a future world of ideas, concepts and viewpoints developed and discussed only by people with whom you have selected to engage – *people who like you.* What will this do to the evolution of our ideas? What will the offspring of our ideas look like?

Of course there is robust debate in the hive of the Internet, but is our world becoming a world of less compromise and harder positions? Are we in fact reinforcing each other in our social networks and then taking those hardened positions out to battle? Is social media and our groups and friends and idea allies giving us a false sense of the "rightness" of our positions? Does it seem to you that political positions are more black and white than ever? Does it appear that religious differences have hardened?

Social media has been credited with bringing oppressed groups together and contributing to the Arab Spring and the Occupy movement. Clearly there are positives to bringing "like" people together. A recent University of Chicago study showed that about one in three marriages start online. Whether they are more satisfying than marriages where people met in person first can be debated, but there is some evidence they are slightly happier. Whether in politics, religion or marriage, I have never seen so little compromise in my whole life as I do now.

It's not only having like-minded people in thought exchanges that could be hurting generations of ideas and our ability to compromise. The social media sites, in an effort to make your experience more worthwhile, actually self-perpetuate your ideas. How do they do that? Who tells you what to read? Who tells you what to watch? In my opinion, "Recommended for You" is one of the most evolutionary steps backward in thought evolution. Theoretically, I am showing you what you already like, something consistent with your "interests" and positions and written by people like you. If we are going to have

"Recommend for You," I would like equal time for five things that will make you say, "What?"

So what can we do to fight back on the "genetic engineering" of ideas and thought leadership?

1. Suspend judgment. Encourage people to consider and integrate contrary thinking at the beginning of any project. This is the cornerstone of brainstorming.

2. Avoid GroupThink. Make sure contrary opinions are welcome. Designate one or two people to serve as devil's advocates. GroupThink was a concept pushed by an article in the *Harvard Business Review* back around the time of the failed Bay of Pigs invasion. How did so many smart people make such a foolish decision?

3. Solicit input from introverts. Ask questions of those who aren't speaking. Introverts may have contrary ideas that are essential, but you will have to prod them to speak. When I studied at the Center for Creative Leadership at the age of 28, I was taught that if you aren't communicating well with an extrovert, you aren't listening. Conversely, if you aren't communicating well with an introvert, you aren't asking.

4. Build diversity into your teams and groups. If you know someone thinks something is a bad idea or has serious concerns with the objectives or methods of a project, make sure he or she is on the project team. Sometimes we build teams with too much functionality. At leadership school we were split into two teams, one with individuals like us and one with people very different from us. The team with very similar people got things done quicker, but the result wasn't as good.

5. Pause before you hit the send button. I have served as president on several homeowner association boards. I am convinced that an HOA board is the best and toughest training for learning compromise and how to deal with people. I have a dear friend who always writes me an email when conversations over hot dogs, or bikes or pools gets overheated and she says, "Hit the 'Pause Button' first." I think we would advance ourselves dramatically if every email in the world was preceded by asking, "Are you really sure you want to send this?" I even imagine a button that requires a reflection period.

I think the issue of whether our mutual reinforcement is affecting our world dialogue and our capacity for compromise is a serious and legitimate question. I am interested especially in hearing from those who disagree with me. The current dialogue about everything imaginable is so uncivil it reminds me of Dan Akroyd and Jane Curtin in Point/Counterpoint from *Saturday Night Live*. "Jane, you ignorant slut." A world where we pick our audiences and our audiences pick us and our thoughts are reinforced with algorithms (along with our buying habits) may produce a weaker future species of ideas and a world of hardened positions.

Remember your Greek mythology? It was Nemesis who led Narcissus to the pool of water where he just stared at himself after he rejected the nymph Echo. We all need nemesis and unpleasantness in our diet—it is healthy for our ideas. In the meantime, I hope LinkedIn will send me some posts that are not "Recommended for You." In the self reinforcing world of social media, we need variety; we need to have some dishes put in front of us that aren't our favorites by people who aren't our friends.

Careers, Retirement, and Mortgages

NOVEMBER 13, 2014

What are you going to do for a career, lad? I remember vividly being asked this question many times. My earliest memories are, in fact, adults asking me this question. And yet, according to a recent Bureau of Labor Statistics Study, the average employee today lasts less than 5 years (4.7, to be exact) at any position. If you are 55-64, however, average tenure is 10.4 years. Now, being 55, I am bombarded with emails and regular mail asking me when I will retire. According to a recent Gallup survey, those planning to retire at 65 have dropped from 49% in 1995 to 26% in 2013. I myself have had numerous 30-year mortgages, but only one lasted longer than 5 years due to the need to move for a job or opportunity. Nevertheless, the 30-year mortgage is still what is used to buy a house or condo.

Is it just me, or are careers, retirement, and mortgages headed towards extinction like the largest dinosaur imaginable?

Notice how careers, retirement, and mortgages are designed to work together. The parents of we Boomers went to work in their 20's after college, got married soon after—very soon after, as the median age for a male to marry in 1956 was 23. It is now 29. Buying that first home in 1960 was something you did at 24 or 25. The average age now is estimated to be early to mid-30's and climbing. Think the home mortgage has been around awhile? Think again. Invented in the 1930's, it didn't catch on until the Federal Housing Administration was formed in 1934. Original mortgages were for half of the house's value and you had a balloon payment after several years.

Down payment?

That could be as much as 80-percent. The FHA lowered payments and made mortgages affordable to help us recover from the Great Depression. Retirement? Who invented that? Well, I will skip German history and tell you that in the United States the Social Security Act was passed in 1937. The concept of career as progression within an organization is itself a 20th century development. Remember that most (97%) of us were farmers or engaged in some aspect of farming at the turn of the century.

Considering how recent the concept of a career, mortgage and retirement are, the question may fairly be asked, "Why keep them?" Are they relevant or are they idealized notions crystallized in the 1950's? A time when you graduated, got married, bought a house, worked to pay it off during your career at the company and then retired off your house equity and pension from your long-term employer. As job tenure trends shorten, who wants to make a 30-year commitment? You won't even have time to cover the transaction costs of buying a home. As the job economy changes so rapidly, who has time to think about a career? Can you even intelligently plan in our current jobs economy? And finally, if you are going to live to be 85-100, what good is the concept of retiring at 65—an age dictated by a generation that only lived to be about 60? The concept of a career, having a 30-year mortgage and retiring; these cornerstones of our recent past are eroding rapidly. What are the replacements, if any?

Here are a few tips to help you consider your future in a world without careers, retirement, and mortgages:

1. Be nimble. Career, retirement, and mortgage are the opposite of what I call, "nimbility." Being too closely tied to these permanent notions is not aligned with our current world.

2. Be open to relocate. The best opportunities may be many miles from where you are now. If you are wedded to a geographic location, you are disadvantaged in the new job economy.

3. If you can't relocate, you can still have mobility. The new "mobile" is the ability to work from anywhere. Be proficient and self-sufficient and consider opportunities allowing you to work from home.

4. *Learn how to learn, think, and solve problems.* Some of the fastest growing professions aren't even 10 years old. Those that get ahead and stay ahead will not be trained in specific languages, they will have learned how to learn.

5. *Think in contingencies.* Don't have a single career plan. Have several. Why? The world is uncertain and changing too rapidly. You are better off with "what if" scenarios than a "certain" plan. If X happens, then I will do Y.

6. *You might need "gobs."* The word "job" comes from "gob," meaning piece. Be comfortable piecing gobs together to create your own "job."

7. *Get a little tenure in your diet somewhere.* A resume where someone moves every year is not a good resume. Have at least one position where you stuck it out for 5 years plus. The average employer imagines it will take 6 months to a year to get you up to speed and a return on recruited investment. Having some tenure shows that if the job is a fit, you are ready, willing and able to commit to an organization.

8. Build a virtual silver cellar. The biggest downside to our current trends is the lack of structured savings. Pensions are dead. Companies have learned they can't have defined benefit plans that guarantee you a certain amount indefinitely when you retire. Longevity has drained and bankrupted those pensions. And, if you don't spend 30-years in a home because you are job hopping and "gobbing," you aren't going to have 30-years of home equity. As a result, failing to have a savings plan for yourself is your biggest risk. So it is urgent and essential that you take advantage of savings program at your company (401k/HSA) or in government sponsored programs (IRA, etc.)

Careers, retirement, and mortgages were designed to solve problems of the 20th century. I personally don't see them surviving much longer. By 2030 we won't be able to pay full benefits on Social Security, job tenure is falling and first time home buying is falling while the median age rises.

American Dream? The picket fence, the organized career, and the retirement home are giving way to a world of survival of the nimble. The biggest risk to the nimble? Hunters and gatherers weren't good at saving—you are going to have to find a way to put something aside and create a virtual silver cellar.

❖ ❖ ❖

1. *Get physical with the people in your life.* While longevity is increasing, I was shocked at how many classmates had already passed on. Eighty or so of the alumni were celebrating on the rooftop of the Moonrise Hotel in University City and we wiped away tears as we viewed pictures of classmates who were deceased. There was a video set to a rendition of "Somewhere Over the Rainbow" by Israel Kamakawiwoʻole, the Hawaiian singer who died at the young age of 39. I am not an emotional type, but just writing about it affects me. I can't get that song and those pictures out of my head. I am "Facebooked" and LinkedIn with some of the reunion attendees, but these tools don't compare to being together –in person—the old-fashioned way. Don't rely only on virtual connections; you will regret it.

2. *Cut back on "friends!" Reduce your virtual relationships and focus on the quality of your core relationships.* LinkedIn and Facebook are always trying to get you to add people. Life goes by fast, much faster than you think. How many friends do you have? How many connections do you have? How many of them do you know? How many have you met in person? ***Stop defining yourself by how many.*** Remember summer camp? If you could just make one new friend, that was a big deal. Because that person was a "real friend" with whom you had shared physical experiences. If there's any truth to *The Social Network* movie based on Zuckerberg's

REFLECTIONS

What I Learned From My 30ᵗʰ Law School Reunion

SEPTEMBER 29, 2014

Virtual Relationships are Overrated!

I am second from the left in a picture taken at the party in St. Louis, Missouri celebrating 30-years since our graduation from Washington University School of Law. I've had no physical contact with the people in the photo since we graduated in 1984. And our times together in law school were relatively undocumented since there was no Internet back then. On the left is Kent, a criminal defense attorney in Kansas City; Sean to my right is a litigator in Milwaukee and to his right is Kevin, a criminal defense attorney in Atlanta. I am a business executive, lawyer, and author who lives in Dallas and Austin, Texas. None of our paths crossed after graduation, and yet we spent time together every day for three years (1981-1984) during incredible, academically stressful circumstances. What did I learn from our brief reunion 30-years later? What points can I pass along after attending this reunion?

invention, Facebook was invented by someone who had no friends. Maybe virtual connections are an easy way out? Think about it....

3. *Don't miss the special occasions because you are too busy.* Don't miss the special events. I missed the wedding of one of my college classmates. I had a legitimate excuse but he has never forgiven me and we now have no relationship. Go to your reunions. Hug your classmates. Go to the weddings and the funerals. These celebrations of life or death fill a very important need within our human nature. Do you know why so many of the religious holidays are celebrated in December? It is because the dates came from pagan rituals, which were centered around the winter solstice. Our early ancestors worshiped the sun and were pretty upset when the days kept getting shorter. They would stay together until the shortest day and the days got longer. Think about it; we still do that today! Home for the holidays!

4. *Take the time to track down a teacher or professor who helped you and tell him or her thanks—in person.* Teachers and professors have a profound impact on you and how you think. One professor was kind enough to tell me I was one of the smartest students he ever had. Of course my immediate reaction was to think that he told every student the same thing. But since we had only seen each other twice in 30 years, I could see in his eyes he meant it. That encounter could not have happened via email. I saw this same professor 18 years after I had graduated and was living in San Francisco. At that time, I asked him what he had learned in 18 years of teaching (his first class was our first class). *He said he had learned that everyone learns differently and you need to figure that out for each student—how he or she learns—in order to help them.* That is worth thinking about. This professor's comments at the reunion inspired me to do better, be better and at this point in my life, mentor others more effectively by understanding how they learn. From our discussions at the reunion, I could tell that the professors sincerely wondered whether they really had an impact on our future lives. Based upon my experience and that of my friends, these professors did have tremendous impact on what, how, and whether we see issues in our future lives. Find them and thank them. Very good for your soul.

5. *Spend some non-verbal time with people.* Non-verbal communication represents something like two thirds of all communication content. That is where we store much of our human side. Our virtual world involves none of that. I suppose Skype and other technologies grab some of it. But that tactile sense of being around and with others is part of what makes us human. I have used Web Ex and other devices, and now, video interviewing is growing. However, seeing pictures of Kent, Sean and Kevin were nothing compared to being with them. Certain non-verbal cues from their gestures triggered memories in me. Seeing how they looked now, recalling their mannerisms and all their personality traits had a terrific impact on me.

6. The Temptation to "Measure Up" is gone after 30 years. While competitiveness may be an issue for people attending reunions only a few years after graduation, that stops after a while. What are you doing? What am I doing? How attractive is your spouse. Yada,.. yada… By your 30th reunion, these points don't matter. Sean was married to Sharon when we were in school. She died of cancer. He had a new wife, a wonderful lady. Kevin talked about his son, so we all discussed our respective children. Nobody could care less about anyone else's financial or career situation. Why? Life has taken over. We weren't competing, we were sharing and caring.

If you want to know the value of showing up and being together go watch people say goodbye at the airport. I travel a lot. I love watching folks say goodbye. Go to the drop-off spot at curbside or right before people pass through security. You will see some of the strongest and longest hugs and kisses you will ever see in your life. There simply is no substitute for being together. In some ways transportation and technology are trade-offs. Maybe we should invest more money and effort to see our loved ones more frequently. Life is short, much shorter than you can imagine when you are young. Start now and get yourself some tickets. Get in the habit of showing up at reunions, weddings, funerals, and holiday gatherings. I am going to cut back on virtual friends and find more ways to give hugs to my "real friends." And to all my teachers and professors, I offer sincere and hearty thanks. I wish I had done better with all that you gave me, but I am determined to try harder.

Who Invented the Wall? Time For Its Return!

JULY 19, 2014

The world witnessed the tragic downing of a Malaysian Airlines flight over Ukraine last year killing all 298 on board. The action was rightfully described by our president as "an outrage of unspeakable proportions." Israel and Hamas have spent the last few months exchanging rocket fire and Israel now has invaded Gaza. Iraq is on the verge of collapse as warring Muslim factions tug at its tenuous foundation. Our border is not secure and we've had to manage the more than 50,000 children who have fled their countries to seek safe haven in the U.S. Civil wars seem to be the new normal in developing countries and countries with high religious fractionalization. The Ukraine and Russian dispute seems to be simmering. What are we to do?

It may be time to return to an age-old remedy—some good, tall impenetrable walls. We used walls for much of human experience to keep peace, following Robert Frost's advice, "Good fences make good neighbors." But at some point, walls went out of style. Most likely it was Reagan who caused us to rethink the use of walls in his battle against communism in the world. In 1987, he spoke at the Brandenburg Gate, which separated Eastern and Western Berlin and Europe. "Tear down this wall" was his now famous quote.

So while we celebrated the tearing down of the Berlin Wall, the wall did serve a purpose for many years. It kept the peace. In any event, it simply does not matter how or when we stopped viewing walls as a good thing. I firmly believe that it is now time to bring back walls. Walls are not simply for our safety and security; they help define to whom we belong. All these thoughts—and a trip to Lucca, Italy last fall—got me to thinking. Who invented the wall and why?

The Internet is a gift to the minds of those who thirst for knowledge. If you hunger for meaning, the Internet will not satisfy that by itself. Travel, on the other hand, is by its nature disruptive and puts us in a position and state of mind to inquire and reflect. A combination of travel and the Internet produces a synergy that leads to meaning as questions arising from disruption can be both stimulated by and answered by searches in the cloud. This is why you can't search for meaning on the Internet. Meaning doesn't come packaged, it is the result of inquiry flowing from dissatisfaction or discombobulating experience.

If you doubt this in any respect, consider how the apple falling on Newton's head led to the "discovery" of gravity. How revered is this process of learning? Well, what does the world's most familiar brand use as its logo? Newton's apple is the symbol of Apple, a company whose mission is to disrupt our view and use of technology.

While I was recently in Tuscany with my wife and some friends, our Florentine driver, Marzio, suggested we visit Lucca, a walled city about forty-minutes by car from Florence. While the area is significant for several reasons, I was most intrigued by the wall that completely enclosed the village. There are two types of old villages in Italy, those from Etruscan times and those built by the Romans. There is a simple rule that tells you what type of village you're in: The Etruscans built high in the hills and mountains for protection. The Romans built in the valleys on rivers. The residents used the rivers as a source of food, energy and, of course, water. But valleys lack the security of the hills, hence the need for walls.

The walls of Lucca were medieval walls, but then were reconstructed during the Renaissance at great effort and expense. Rebuilding the wall of Lucca required the destruction of two churches and all the hamlets in the outer vicinity of the walls. The walls are imposing and remain in good condition to this day. The Luchese Wall is a wide thoroughfare with a road in the middle. We walked the Luchese Wall and read signs providing information about the history as well as safety. There was also a notation that the wall served as a means of self-identification. There wasn't any detailed explanation, but I began to think about why someone would have invented the wall.

I couldn't find an answer to this question online. What early man came out of a cave and felt the need to build a wall? Did he or she just start setting rocks down and after a while said, "You can't come to my side of these rocks." Was it a simple binary choice of my side vs. your side thinking? And since the wall had a builder/owner, did that person consciously decide who could come on their side and who couldn't? I don't imagine the first wall being for safety and security, I imagine, being as social as humans are, it defined who was allowed in and provided that all-important sense of belonging and exclusivity.

If you doubt my theory regarding the origin of walls, consider the popularity of Facebook. Arguably, the process of creating an account and picking friends is a wall-building process. But I am getting ahead of myself.

While the Luchese Wall certainly had as a purpose securing its citizens in their valley, it also served a social function. As we walked around the wall, you could see evidence of the social aspect of the wall as a promenade and place to gather and share. The sign mentioned that in defiance of the military purpose, the citizens would stroll the top of the wall. On the beautiful day we visited Lucca, it was lunchtime and the wall was occupied with local joggers, people having lunch, and parents walking with their children.

The uses of the Lucca wall for leisure reinforce the social aspects of walls. As I see it, the inventor of the wall was one of the first to embrace binary logic. There are only two sides of the wall. Which side are you on? The ancient inventor preceded George Boole, the founder of Boolean logic and computational thinking, and used the wall to distinguish "this not that." Within his pioneer work in the field, Boole reduced all logic to three possibilities: and, or and not. In a social context, it meant you belonged to those on your side of the wall. Walls don't just keep others out. They help those inside experience a sense of belonging and self-identify.

Interesting citizens have lived inside the wall of Lucca. The village is the birthplace of Carlo Collodi, author of Pinocchio, and Giacomo Puccini, the famous Italian composer whose operas include *La Boheme, Madame Butterfly, Tosca* and many others.

Puccini's operas are among the most commonly performed, and he competes with Verdi for the title of greatest Italian composer. I recall seeing *La Boheme* for the first time and worrying about being able to follow the story. I asked a gentleman behind me who seemed to know his way around an opera house, "What happens?"

He said, "You will see." I prodded him further. Clearly an ancestor to the wall inventor, he said simply, "They fall in love." And sure enough, they did. Before the second act, I asked, "What next?" He said, "She gets sick." And, sure enough, she did. I only had to look at him before the final act and he said, "She dies." And she did. Observe the beauty of the simplicity. In love, not in love; well or sick; alive or dead. Think how easily these binary states can drive plots. Which side of the wall are you on?

Pinocchio is the ultimate binary character, I suppose. When he tells the truth, all is well. But when he lies, his nose grows and everyone knows that he is lying. While our modern thinking recognizes, rightly or wrongly, shades of truth, Pinocchio's nose takes away the doubt. And the original book was called, *The Misadventures of Pinocchio*, indicating all the troubles he caused. Surely his mishaps would have been prevented by a good wall like the wall of Lucca, where author Carlo Claudio was born.

In any event, whoever invented the first wall put humanity on a path that led to the wall of Lucca, a wall that both secured inhabitants and property and provided identity. As you walk along that broad road at the top of the wall on a pretty fall day, as I did, you feel the pride among the people of Lucca and the sense of belonging that the wall provides.

It is this same sense of belonging and exclusivity in the

physical form of a wall that exists today in virtual form on the Internet on sites like Facebook. We decide who we friend and others friend us. While you can't see the wall, it is as strong and as powerful as the wall of Lucca. Yes, we only want to share our lives with our friends and not with strangers. Privacy is the security aspect of the virtual Internet wall. But there is also the social and belonging aspect as we post. And what do we post on? We post on each other's "walls."

What made Zuckerberg's invention powerful was not his programming. He tapped into a fundamental human need. It was the need we have for a wall, our wall, and our need to share walls with those we love and those we choose and trust. Perhaps the Facebook phenomenon shows that we miss the villages our ancestors lived in and the walls, like the one in Lucca, that we shared.

As we watch chaos unfold in front of us from so many places in the world and we witness death and destruction, we must ask ourselves whether the idealism that tore down the Berlin Wall needs to give way to a different reality. It was the reality that Robert Frost observed: "Good fences make good neighbors." When positions are binary, as they are in Israel/Hamas, Russian/Ukraine, Sunni/Shia and the list goes on, why not a binary solution? When the Berlin Wall came down, it was a symbol indicating that Europe was ready to reunite and that transparency and reform were ready to blossom. But that was then and this is now.

We face new and strong hatred that needs time to work itself out on the other side of the wall. As Frost suggests, spring is a time for mending fences, i.e., rebuilding them.

In Reagan's speech at the Brandenburg Gate, he quotes an author who wrote on the wall in spray paint, speculating that it was written by a young Berliner, "This wall will fail." But until we can learn to live together more peacefully, I am afraid I have to agree with Frost's neighbor. It is time to build and mend fences—until enough time passes and a child someday can say, "This wall will fail." The world, it seems to me, needs a "time-out." Sometimes hatred just needs to die off. Until then, however, you will find me on my side of the wall.

When We Leave the Home of the Brave

JULY 4, 2014

Happy Fourth of July to all my fellow citizens of our incredible country! Thanks and God bless the troops and leaders who secured our liberty, the veterans who preserved it, and the soldiers who, while we celebrate, protect us at home and abroad. We are a grateful nation.

I was inspired to write this article by friends I have acquired by way of being an empty nester. We're now living in a couple of large, very full nests of folks in what we call *high-rise* condominiums. These buildings are akin to great birdhouses. The two buildings in Texas, where I own condos, are occupied by people who have been lucky in life. They can afford to travel extensively, and do so often. I was reminded of just how much they travel when one of our friends in Austin made a typical Fourth of July request: "Hey, who wants to grab some fried chicken this weekend?" This was not just any fried chicken. One of our neighbors had bought a Gus's chicken franchise. What could be more American than fried chicken with neighbors on the Fourth of July!

But regrets flowed in rapidly. One friend was in London, another in Berlin, another in Paris, some were in Vail and I myself was on a golf trip with some buddies in Cancun. What were we all doing celebrating July 4th abroad? Celebrating the right to travel. The right to travel is a hidden right. You won't find it in the Constitution, exactly. I checked. You won't find it in the Declaration of Independence. I checked there, too. I suppose you could throw it under some broad Pursuit of Happiness concept. But the right to travel abroad is an inherent right. The power to travel and the instructions to those we encounter abroad appears in a document I bet you have never read— your passport.

Maybe it's my legal background, but every July 4th I read the Constitution and its amendments and the Declaration of Independence. I highly recommend it—it's full of interesting nuances. Why does the president have to be 35-years old, but to be a senator you only have to be 30? I'll have to look that up someday. And these guys could write! How about this line from the Declaration of Independence: "A Prince whose character is thus marked by every act which may define a Tyrant, is unfit to be the ruler of a free people." You have to believe that really set off King George when he read it.

This year, inspired by the RSVP's that flowed in from all over the world, I read my passport as well. On the first page it has a portion from the Star-Spangled Banner,

"O say does that Star-Spangled Banner yet wave, O'er the land of the free and the home of the brave..."

And on the next page a quote from Abraham Lincoln:

"...AND THAT GOVERNMENT OF THE PEOPLE, BY THE PEOPLE, FOR THE PEOPLE, SHALL NOT PERISH FROM THE EARTH."

And then finally what follows on page two is what makes the right to travel possible.

"The Secretary of State of the United States of America hereby requests all whom it may concern to permit the citizen/national of the United States named herein to pass without delay or hindrance and in case of need to give all lawful aid and protection."

Despite all the years I handed my passport to foreign states and hotels, I don't believe I ever really studied it. Certainly not as much as I did today. Wherever we are this July 4th, our great country is looking after us and our passports say in effect, let this citizen pass freely and help him or her if they need it. That's just cool.

The third and fourth pages of the passport have your

personal information and the beginning of the Declaration of Independence. The picture on the fourth page is striking. It depicts one mean looking bald eagle, as if to say, "if you don't take good care of our citizen/national, you will have us to reckon with."

I will skip the more routine instructions in the ensuing pages of the passport and end with a quote from someone you or I probably have never heard of, Ellison S. Onizuka. The name is located on the last page of the passport. His quote: "Every generation has the obligation to free men's minds for a look at new worlds... To look out from a higher plateau than the last generation."

So who was Ellison Onizuka? I had to look it up. He was a U.S. astronaut from Hawaii. Based on what I read, an incredible human being. He was a lieutenant colonel in the Air Force and died in January 1986 when the space shuttle Challenger was destroyed in flight. Another one of our veterans who died in a different kind of mission. A mission to find "higher plateaus."

The right to travel abroad, to literally expand our horizons and be a part of the larger world may not have been anticipated by our founders, but our country was founded by those who traveled abroad for a better life. As Americans, we are inherently mobile and driven to find the "higher plateau," Ellison Onizuka notes in his quote on the last page of our passports. Happy Fourth of July from

Cancun, QRoo, Mexico. And God Bless the United States of America!

❖ ❖ ❖

An Ode to Bill McCabe

DECEMBER 2013

God has rounded up Bill McCabe. News of Bill's illness and death in Northern California reached me in Texas by way of our mutual friend and my former law partner, Jay Strauss. Jay inquired of Bill's friends whether there would be a memorial of any kind at The RoundUp Saloon. It's the biker bar in Lafayette, California that Bill owned and managed when I met him in 1994 but which he had long since sold in favor of a sheep ranch. If there was a tougher and more grisly entrepreneur in NorCal, I never met him. But what I loved about Bill wasn't just his gritty strut and aggressive carriage, it was his yarn spinning. Think John Wayne meets Mark Twain.

As with most people or things, first impressions are powerful and Bill was no exception. My first encounter with Bill was in 1994 in connection with the Lafayette Chamber of Commerce. Through an effort to get my family closer to my ailing and dying father in San Diego, I had relocated to the Bay Area. Here I'd landed a consulting and legal opportunity. As that opportunity wound down, I started an HR outsourcing venture headquartered in Lafayette. To the dismay of several of the upper-class citizens and business owners, the owner of the smelly, rundown biker bar, Bill McCabe, had gotten himself elected President of the Lafayette Chamber of Commerce. Wanting to immediately connect with the city, I threw my hat in the ring for an available seat on that humble board.

In that time and place, voting was by paper ballot.My brother Scott and I took to the streets and we were handing out ballots when we happened upon the Round Up. Bill, who we had only heard of, came scrambling out of his office, took one look at the ballots and in a shrill voice said, "Cease and desist! Cease and desist!" He explained that the ballots were carefully marked, and ours would ruin the entire election. While we knew that wasn't true, we were persuaded that Bill believed it to be true. After a civil conversation, we ordered a beer and worked it out. Bill didn't drink as I recall, and having represented many Chicago restaurants as a corporate lawyer, I was familiar with the occupational hazard of alcoholism in the bar and restaurant industry.

Cease and desist aside, I was elected to the Chamber Board. The first order of business was a retreat to the Monterey Coast. As outgoing president, in the shadows of 100-year old redwoods, our local saloon owner gave a speech on entrepreneurship that captured its essence. Bill delivered it like a preacher who had tasted deeply elements of the rough and tumble world; an eloquent junkyard dog giving a poetic sermon.

"We are all crazy, crazy like nuts," he began in that firm but shrill voice. "I mean we all need our heads examined. There is a cruise ship and everyone else is on it. We are not. We are the idiots in sea kayaks. On the cruise ship everything is provided for you. You get meals. You get snacks. You get entertainment. There is a bar. You are waited on. Everything is scheduled. You get to sleep. You get your laundry done, your bags carried. There is a spa and social and happy hours. Food and fun are plentiful. And where are we? In a sea kayak, alone. And the food gets wet and all we do is row and try to stay alive. And while we row, they sleep. And no one does anything for us. We are crazy, we are nuts."

He continued, "We ought to have our heads examined, we sea kayakers. We could be on that cruise ship with the others. We could live normal lives and be secure and safe and dry and sleeping. But no. We won't hear of it. We want to feel the waves. We want to feel the pain. We want to hunger and we want to thirst. We want to struggle. We want to drown. We want to tempt failure and death." He went on at great length along the same theme. When he finally grew weary or depleted his vocabulary, he stopped abruptly. He stared slowly at each of us and finally said just the word "THERE" and sat down. Nobody knew what to say, leaving us in silence for several minutes while we just took it all in.

But Bill's preaching skills were no match for his ability to tell a story; stories with deep meaning that had purpose behind them, but had humor as well. Satire comes to mind as a theme, and that is why Twain comes to my mind when I remember Bill. His best stories were about his sheep farm. From the stories, it was apparent that Bill was an amateur sheep farmer. Here is one of my favorites—please read it with a gruff, yet shrill voice.

It seems there was a sheep that Bill's wife was particularly fond of; it had been injured somehow, either a bad hip or leg. On a farm, these things happen and the animal is "harvested" for meat. But not this sheep, it was a favorite, it had a name. So, although it made no financial or economic sense, Bill and his wife carted the sheep off to the vet. They stayed in the back of the truck with it and held it. The vet, for a few thousand dollars, fixed the sheep's injury. Bill's wife spent weeks, maybe a month nursing it back to health. Eventually, the sheep was healthy enough to return to the flock. Thousands of dollars, hours of sleepless nights and tender loving care and what happened? Within days it was killed and eaten by a bear.

Recently, I told that story to a manager who'd fallen in love with the work of an employee. Afterward, I told him, "Don't get too attached and bet too much of the farm on one employee." Shit happens. I think Bill would have liked that.

Here is another sheep story:

Bill and his wife were going to be gone from the farm for a while, so he put all the sheep in the barn to keep them away from the bears, wolves and coyotes. He wanted them to be safe. Dogs protected and herded the sheep when they were outside and Bill thought he should put the guardian dogs in with them too. It sounded perfectly logical and he thought nothing of it. Upon their return, he opened the door to find a couple of panting and smiling dogs, along with a bunch of dead sheep. Apparently the dogs tried to herd the sheep in that confined space and ran them round and round until they died of exhaustion. Why were the dogs smiling? They thought they had done a good job. None of the sheep had gotten away. There are plenty of morals in that story.

There were many other great stories surrounding the bar itself, including a misunderstanding that I was sadly a small part of surrounding a birthday party and perhaps some alcohol. My friend's son was having a birthday party and we were in the RoundUp having a pre-party and doing some planning. There were a couple of young girls in the bar about the age of my friend's son. We invited them to the party and they politely declined. My friend then went too far and offered to pay for them to come. Well you can imagine what happened. The two girls were daughters of friends of Bill. And sure enough I got a call from Bill who wanted a "sit down." It turns out, by the time the story made its way to Bill, my friend was (wrongly of course) accused of propositioning the girls with money for some questionable purpose. Bill was furious, but he viewed my friend as naive and maybe not aware of his error. But then Bill gazed at me and said, "But you, you Cash, you know your way around a 'gin bar'. Why didn't you do something?" There was nothing to say that would make him happy and I knew better than to argue with him. So I just said, "Sorry Bill." He considered banning us from the RoundUp, but then he thought better of it. He still glared at me for a month or two. As a man of the world, I suppose I was somehow accountable.

I sort of wish I had been banned from the RoundUp for a while—what an honor that would have been. And Bill, safe travels to the great beyond. I will soon travel to Lafayette with my brother to meet with friends and toast your unique and warm impact on our lives and souls.

The Walking Smile,
An Ode to My High School Chum

OCTOBER 21, 2014

I attended Central School in a tiny hamlet tucked into the Adirondack foothills, a place that now makes for distant but fond memories. It was in that small village, Mohawk, New York, where a significant stone in the foundation of my youth was laid. While the memory in its entirety is shrouded by so many years of events, there are nevertheless aspects that live large in my mind's eye. The sound of a fan-packed gym during a basketball game, the smell of fall, damp leaves blending with fresh smoke, and the never ending broad smile of my friend, Mark Woroby. These memories are timeless in their presentation, and continue to affect me as if they are happening now. Even as I sit in urban Dallas, staring at the night traffic from twelve stories up, those images never seems to fade.

I learned late today that the Mohican smile so bigger than life will not be seen again in person by me or anyone else because my high school chum, Mark Woroby, has died. News of Mark's death flowed across the miles, mostly via Facebook, through classmates from Mohawk Central School, who by now have mostly migrated to other states. We had a decent turnout in Cooperstown in 2002 for our 25th reunion. Mark, of course was the MC of our gathering as he was a unifier, a gifted speaker, and a motivated fundraiser. He spent most of his life raising money for noble and needy causes. His last position was to turn around the financial prospects of the Make A Wish Foundation of Northeast New York.

My closest memories of Mark probably involved basketball. Nearly forty years later, I recall as high school freshmen, how we shared the horrible distinction of not winning a single game. What a waste of new Converse™ sneakers. It was depressing to say the least. But I remember so clearly that never-ending smile and positive and infectious winning attitude that Mark carried to lead us through. As a practical matter, the best freshmen players played JV ball while those of us who were just "okay" floundered on the freshman team. Mark was our point guard. As disappointing and tough as it was to play and be drubbed every week, Mark and the team would bring the ball down the court and try and try again. Other schools cared about their freshman team. I guess our school focused on JV and Varsity. Mark carried us emotionally. It wasn't easy, but we learned some important lessons that season, including handling failure and trying in the face of extreme adversity.

Somewhere along the way, he got the nickname, The Sheik—someone will have to remind me why, but I think it had to do with a towel. There were countless stories that will take me time to remember, and without a doubt these will surface in my dreams over the next several nights. As all our encounters were positive, I know they will be pleasant dreams of a special soul. Mark is somewhere else now, helping the less fortunate, carrying the needy through difficult times, and inspiring others to do their best even when the odds are dim.

For those of us left to carry on, the best we can do is fund a scholarship in Mark's memory at Mohawk Central. The scholarship will support the college education of someone seeking a life similar to the one Mark led. And although we will work to encourage those souls, they will not replace our dear classmate, may his smiling and loving soul be put to use by God in another place.

EPILOGUE: GETTING TO NEXT

Some major takeaways from my writing, which I think have helped me in my career, are 1) stay curious 2) assertively engage others 3) reflect on major life events 4) don't assume all progress is forward progress and 5) keep moving forward. Doing things like studying young children while their brains are forming (*Six Learning Tips from a Six-Month Old*) and attending *Summer Camp at 55* are examples of staying young. Remain engaged by watching and doing things that young people do. These actions and activities by themselves will keep you curious and learning. And those who commit to lifelong learning are those who succeed.

Whether a career takes you on the road or not, assertively engage with others. It will bring depth to your life and your thinking. Thought leadership doesn't happen late at night when you are alone. It comes from actively engaging with others and hashing out your viewpoints. Meeting strangers is disruptive. But as you read in *Who Invented the Wall*, you will know the power of disruption as it applies to the advancement of understanding. I will never forget my monk! And remember, Ross Perot. He was a greeter in the Navy, which eventually led him to his first job at IBM. He assertively engaged an IBM'er, and it led to billions in earnings.

When good and bad things happen—a promotion or the loss of a loved one—take time to express yourself. If you don't want to write about the experience, then simply talk about it with someone. Loss is a learning experience and studies show that you cope better if you share your feelings. Losing my dear high school chum this year was tough, but recalling his smile has made me smile more since. Remember Dale Carnegie's tips from *How to Win Friends and Influence People*? Smile was one of his top pieces of advice. Smiling is great for your success.

As social media grows, some of the unintended consequences will become more obvious. An Internet friend is not the same as a personal engagement. I recall when studying philosophy that the great empiricist, David Hume, basically said, "There is a difference between eating a hot dog and thinking about eating a hot dog." The virtual world is overrated, as I recount and recall from my *What I Learned from My 30th High School Reunion* essay. Most social media communication is non-verbal. Conversely, successful people show up and engage others face to face.

But while reflecting on life, trends, and loss have their

place, the most important tip of all is to keep moving forward. You will skin your knee. You will fail. You will suffer loss. Some days you won't feel like getting out of bed. But life is short. In an effort to motivate me to get up and work on the farm, my grandfather always said, "Most people die in their sleep." So live in the present, take it one day at a time, but keep moving forward. Don't dwell on bucket lists, tasting every small bite. Get yourself some steak. Success comes from depth, not dabbling. ❖

ACKNOWLEDGEMENTS

I want to thank my book team, which is blazing a trail in the new world of publishing. This includes Steve Bennett and his associates at AuthorBytes, David Ratner of Ratner PR and Johanna Ramos Boyer. I also want to thank those who have read and commented on my essays, which consist primarily of my neighbors in Dallas and Austin and my wife, Evie, who finds a way to like everything I write, yet is a perfect critic when it comes to providing constructive feedback.

Steven Cash Nickerson

BIOGRAPHY

Cash Nickerson is President and a Principal of PDS Tech, Inc., a position he has held for 11 years. With over $400 million in annual sales, PDS is one of the largest engineering and IT staffing firms in the United States, employing over 10,000 employees annually.   He has held a variety of legal and executive positions in his 30 year career including serving as an attorney and marketing executive for Union Pacific Railroad, an associate and then partner at Jenner & Block, one of Chicago's five largest law firms and chairman and CEO of an Internet company he took public through a reverse merger.

An avid writer and speaker on employment, Mr. Nickerson is the author of the recently published, critically acclaimed book on employment, *StagNation, Understanding the New Normal in Employment.* (2013) And, the recently published book, *BOOMERangs, Engaging the Aging Workforce in America* (2014). He also writes travel books including *A Texan in Tuscany* (2013).

Mr. Nickerson holds a JD and MBA from Washington University in St. Louis where he was an editor of the law review and a recipient of the US Steel Scholarship. He is a member of the National Council of the Washington University in St. Louis School of Law and International Council of the Whitney R. Harris World Law Institute. Mr. Nickerson serves on the Equifax Workforce Solutions Client Advisory Board and was Keynote speaker at the Equifax 2013 Client Forum. Mr. Nickerson was honored with the Distinguished Alumni Award in 2013 by Washington University in St. Louis School of Law. He received the Global Philanthropy Award in 2010 from Washington University in St. Louis for his support of the Crimes Against Humanity Initiative. Mr. Nickerson was elected the Ethan A. H. Shepley Trustee at Washington University in St. Louis on December 5, 2014 for a four year term.

Mr. Nickerson is licensed to practice law in California, Nevada, Illinois, Nebraska and Texas and is a member of the American, Los Angeles and Dallas Bar Associations. He is an avid martial artist, ranked as a third degree black belt in Kenpo Karate, and he is a Russian Martial Art instructor at his school, Big D Systema in Dallas.

Mr. Nickerson has appeared on numerous talk radio shows, including NPR, The Joe Elliot Show, Americas Evening News, Lifestyle Talk Radio, The Lifestyle Show, Conversations with Peter Solomon, Ringside Politics, The Dave Malarkey Show and The Morning Show, NPR.

Made in the USA
Middletown, DE
23 April 2015